LBJ Library photo by Elizabeth Shoumatoff

Lady Bird Johnson

FIRST LADY

LADY BIRD JOHNSON

1912–2007

MEMORIAL TRIBUTES

IN THE

ONE HUNDRED TENTH CONGRESS OF THE UNITED STATES

Senate Document 110–8

U.S. GOVERNMENT PRINTING OFFICE

WASHINGTON : 2008

For sale by the Superintendent of Documents, U.S. Government Printing Office
Internet: bookstore.gpo.gov   Phone: toll free (866) 512–1800; DC area (202) 512–1800
Fax: (202) 512–2250   Mail: Stop SSOP, Washington, DC 20402–0001

ORDER FOR PRINTING OF TRIBUTES AND STATEMENTS

FRIDAY, *July 13, 2007*

Ms. KLOBUCHAR. Mr. President, I ask unanimous consent that a collection of statements made in tribute to the late First Lady of the United States, LADY BIRD JOHNSON, together with appropriate illustrations and other materials relating to her death be printed.

The PRESIDING OFFICER. Without objection, it is so ordered.

Compiled under the direction
of the
Joint Committee on Printing

CONTENTS

BIOGRAPHY

Wife, mother, grandmother, conservationist, businesswoman, philanthropist, First Lady. LADY BIRD JOHNSON holds claim to all of those titles and more.

All her life, Mrs. JOHNSON has brought beauty to her sprawling family, to the Texas hill country she loves, and to the Nation that loves her.

She inspired the passage of the Beautification Act of 1965—a bill her husband called a "gift" to his wife—which cemented environmentalism as a top priority in the United States. Married for four decades to one of the most powerful men in the world, Mrs. JOHNSON juggled extraordinarily demanding jobs as her husband's closest advisor as he rose from Congressman to Senator to Vice President to President and as mother to daughters Lynda Bird and Luci Baines. After her husband's death, she spent the next three and a half decades solidifying all that she had laid in place during their marriage.

Today, LADY BIRD JOHNSON's legacy lives on in the millions of blooms planted in the Nation's Capital, in the sweeping banks of wildflowers lining U.S. highways, and in the charm of Austin's revitalized Town Lake. An equally lasting legacy is her extraordinary family—Lynda Johnson Robb and her husband Charles; Luci Baines Johnson and her husband Ian Turpin; 6 granddaughters and 1 grandson; and 10 great-grandchildren.

Mrs. JOHNSON was born CLAUDIA ALTA TAYLOR in the East Texas town of Karnack on December 22, 1912. Her father, Thomas Jefferson Taylor, was owner of a general store. Her mother, Minnie Pattillo Taylor, died when CLAUDIA was 5 years old, leaving the little girl and her two older brothers, Tommy and Tony, in the care of their father and their Aunt Effie. Legend has it that a nursemaid said CLAUDIA was "as purty as a LADY BIRD"; the sweet nickname suited her and stuck for life.

Mrs. JOHNSON graduated from Marshall High School in 1928 and attended Saint Mary's Episcopal School for Girls in Dallas from 1928 to 1930. She then entered the University of Texas at Austin, graduating in 1933 with a bachelor of arts in history and in 1934, with a bachelor of journalism with honors.

She met the tall, ambitious man whom she would marry when he was a congressional secretary visiting Austin on official business. Lyndon Baines Johnson courted LADY BIRD TAYLOR with all the single-minded energy he would later bring to elected office. They were engaged just 7 weeks after their first date and married in November 1934. Mrs. JOHNSON recalled that "sometimes Lyndon simply [took] your breath away." Her life with Lyndon Johnson was one of such achievement in politics, business and philanthropy it left those around them breathless, too.

Mrs. JOHNSON was independently a successful businesswoman. In 1943, she bought a failing low-power daytime-only Austin radio station with an inheritance from her mother. Armed with her journalism degree and a tireless work ethic, she took a hands-on ownership role, selling advertising, hiring staff, and even cleaning floors. Over time, her Austin broadcasting company grew to include an AM and FM radio station and a television station, all bearing the same call letters: KTBC. The family later expanded the LBJ holdings to stations in Waco and Corpus Christi and a cable television system. After selling the television station in 1972 and the cable system in the early 1990s, the family grew their radio interests in Austin to include six stations. Mrs. JOHNSON stayed actively involved in the LBJ Holding Company well into her eighties.

LADY BIRD JOHNSON is probably best known for her support of her husband's career. When Lyndon Johnson volunteered for the U.S. Navy in World War II, Mrs. JOHNSON ran his congressional office, serving constituents' needs in every way except voting. Her support for her husband's political career continued throughout his years in government. She campaigned actively for his race for the Congress, Senate, Vice Presidency and Presidency. In 1960, she covered 35,000 miles for the Kennedy/Johnson ticket, and in 1964, she campaigned independently on a whistle-stop train throughout the South for the Johnson/Humphrey ticket. President Johnson paid her the highest of compliments, saying he thought that the voters "would happily have supported her over me."

LADY BIRD JOHNSON stood by her husband on the fateful November day in 1963 when Lyndon Johnson became the 36th President of the United States after the assassination of John Kennedy. Her official White House biography notes that her gracious personality and Texas hospitality did much to heal the pain of those dark days. She created a First Lady's Committee for a More Beautiful Capital and then expanded her program to include the entire Nation. She was also highly involved in the President's War on Poverty, focusing in particular on Project Head Start for preschool children.

While President Johnson was still in office, Mrs. JOHNSON played a key role in the plans to build the LBJ Library and Museum and the LBJ School of Public Affairs in Austin, TX. The library is in the process of building the Lady Bird Johnson Center, consisting of educational classrooms and outdoor landscaping. After the Johnsons' White House years ended in 1969, Mrs. JOHNSON authored "A White House Diary," a memoir that drew on her considerable skills as a writer and historian. "I was keenly aware that I had a unique opportunity, a front row seat, on an unfolding story and nobody else was going to see it from quite the vantage point that I saw it." She also co-authored "Wildflowers Across America" with Carlton Lees.

In December 1972, President and Mrs. JOHNSON gave the LBJ Ranch house and surrounding property to the people of the United States as a national historic site.

On her 70th birthday in 1982, Mrs. JOHNSON founded the National Wildflower Research Center, a nonprofit environmental organization dedicated to the preservation and re-establishment of native plants in natural and planned landscapes. She donated funding and 60 acres of land in Austin to establish the organization. In December 1997, the property was renamed the Lady Bird Johnson Wildflower Center in honor of Mrs. JOHNSON's 85th birthday. In 2006, the Lady Bird Johnson Wildflower Center became a part of the University of Texas at Austin, guaranteeing its permanent place in the national landscape—and ensuring that LADY BIRD JOHNSON's name will live on in the hearts of Americans.

As a child, LADY BIRD JOHNSON paddled in the dark bayous of Caddo Lake in East Texas under ancient cypress trees decorated with Spanish moss. The sense of place that came from being close to the land never left her. She would devote much of her life to preserving it.

As she was growing up, earning her degrees from the University of Texas at Austin and tending to the many duties as wife of a rising political star, Mrs. JOHNSON often noted the impact that natural beauty had on her life. But she was First Lady of the Nation before she was able to translate her love for the land into national policy. Once started, she amassed a lifetime of achievement as the "Environmental First Lady."

Former Secretary of the Interior Stewart Udall credits several trips to the American West, the Rocky Mountains and Utah with igniting Mrs. JOHNSON's interest in conservation. In 1964, when she visited Indian reservations and dedicated the Flaming Gorge Dam in Utah, she told audiences that natural beauty was their greatest resource and must be protected.

Right after the 1964 election, she decided that "the whole field of conservation and beautification" had the greatest appeal to her.

Soon after that, she was urging her husband to see what could be done about junkyards along the Nation's highways.

Today, perhaps, most people think of LADY BIRD JOHNSON as the reason why we see wildflowers blooming along the Nation's highways and fewer junkyards and billboards. The Beautification Act of 1965 was one tangible result of Mrs. JOHNSON's campaign for national beautification. Known as "Lady Bird's bill" because of her active support, the legislation called for control of outdoor advertising, including removal of certain types of signs along the Nation's interstate system and the existing Federal-aid primary system. It also required certain junkyards along interstate or primary highways to be removed or screened and encouraged scenic enhancement and roadside development.

It is part of that legacy that today the Surface Transportation and Uniform Relocation Assistance Act of 1987 requires that at least one-fourth of 1 percent of funds expended for landscaping projects in the highway system be used to plant native flowers, plants and trees.

The term beautification concerned Mrs. JOHNSON, who feared it was cosmetic and trivial. She emphasized that it meant much more—"clean water, clean air, clean roadsides, safe waste disposal and preservation of valued old landmarks as well as great parks and wilderness areas." Meg Greenwood, writing in the *Reporter*, noted the "deceptively sweet and simple-sounding name of 'beautification'."

Mrs. JOHNSON made it her mission to call attention to the natural beauty of the Nation, and one of her most important efforts was in Washington, DC, which was much in need of a facelift.

In 1964 Mrs. JOHNSON formed the Committee for a More Beautiful Capital, responding to Mary Lasker's suggestion that she make Washington, DC, a "garden city" and a model for the rest of the Nation. Soon afterward Mrs. Lasker, a philanthropist who lobbied for medical research as well as for natural beauty and Mrs. JOHNSON founded the Society for a More Beautiful National Capital, which received private donations for the project. The first planting took place on the Mall where Mrs. JOHNSON planted pansies. She then planted azaleas and dogwood in the triangle at Third and Independence Avenue and ended her first planting effort at a public housing project.

Mrs. JOHNSON enlisted a stellar team to attack the issue, including Nash Castro, White House liaison for the National Park Service, philanthropist Laurance S. Rockefeller, Kathleen Louchheim, an Assistant Secretary of State and leader among Democratic women, and many others.

Mrs. JOHNSON's view of this project went far beyond planting daffodil bulbs. She was concerned with pollution, urban decay, recreation, mental health, public transportation, and the crime rate. The committee agreed to plant flowers in triangle parks all over the city, to give awards for neighborhood beautification, and to press for the revitalization of Pennsylvania Avenue and the preservation of Lafayette Park. The committee also generated enormous donations of cash and azaleas, cherry trees, daffodils, dogwood and other plants in evidence today in Washington's lovely parks and green spaces. Perhaps most important, Mrs. JOHNSON's effort prompted businesses and others to begin beautification efforts in low-income neighborhoods hidden from the much-visited tourist attractions.

One of her key efforts was to clean up trash and control rats in the Shaw section of Washington. That developed into Project Pride, which enlisted Howard University students and high school students to clean up neighborhoods. Mrs. JOHNSON funded the project with a $7,000 grant from the Society for a More Beautiful Capital.

Later, Mrs. JOHNSON was a key player in the White House Conference on Natural Beauty that convened in May 1966, and was coordinated by Laurance S. Rockefeller. She opened the conference with a question: "Can a great democratic society generate the drive to plan, and having planned, execute projects of great natural beauty?" The conference sparked similar local conferences and added momentum to the national conservation movement.

One result was the President's Council on Recreation and Natural Beauty, chaired by Vice President Hubert Humphrey, another vehicle for spreading the conservation message and encouraging such local efforts as anti-litter campaigns.

President Johnson also issued a proclamation declaring 1967 a "Youth Natural Beauty and Conservation Year." The Johnsons opened the year with a press conference honoring youth leaders at the LBJ Ranch.

One method Mrs. JOHNSON employed in her beautification campaign was to call attention to important sites by visiting those places with the media in tow. She visited historic sites, national parks, and scenic areas, usually accompanied by Nash Castro of the National Park Service, a number of dignitaries and the media. Her nine beautification trips included Virginia historic places, the Hudson River in New York, Big Bend National Park and the California Redwoods.

Mrs. JOHNSON's views, expressed in letters and conversations, had influence in preventing the construction of dams in the Grand Canyon and in creating Redwoods National Park.

That the Johnson administration was the most active in conservation since the time of Theodore Roosevelt and Franklin D. Roosevelt is largely due to Mrs. JOHNSON. Among the major legislative initiatives were the Wilderness Act of 1964, the Land and Water Conservation Fund, the Wild and Scenic Rivers Program and many additions to the National Park System, a total of 200 laws relevant to the environment.

The President thanked his wife for her dedication on July 26, 1968, after signing the Department of the Interior appropriations bill. He presented her with 50 pens used to sign some 50 laws relating to conservation and beautification and a plaque that read: "To LADY BIRD, who has inspired me and millions of Americans to try to preserve our land and beautify our Nation. With love from Lyndon."

Just before President Johnson left office, Columbia Island in the Potomac River was renamed Lady Bird Johnson Park. Starting in 1969, Mrs. JOHNSON served on the Advisory Board on National Parks, Historic Sites, Buildings and Monuments.

After leaving Washington, Mrs. JOHNSON focused her efforts on Texas. She was the leading force behind Austin's beautiful hike and bike trail that winds more than 10 miles around the Town Lake portion of the Colorado River, graced with blooming native trees and plants. "She'll say she got on a moving train, but she had the leadership to say it could be a jewel," said Carolyn Curtis, a close family friend. "Now it is the meeting point of all of Austin. It brought in the Hyatt and the Four Seasons. She was the one with that vision."

For 20 years, starting in 1969, she encouraged the beautification of Texas highways by personally giving awards to the highway districts that used native Texas plants and scenery to the best advantage. Her focus was on the ecological advantages as well as the beauty of native plants—a passion that would lead her to create the National Wildflower Research Center in 1982 on the occasion of her 70th birthday.

Mrs. JOHNSON enlisted her friend, actress Helen Hayes, and made a personal contribution of $125,000 and 60 acres east of Austin to start the center, which grew into an organization of more than 13,000 members. The center soon became a national leader in research, education and projects that encouraged the use of wildflowers.

Several years later, Mrs. JOHNSON foresaw the need for a larger site and located a lovely 43-acre piece of land in the hill country of Southwest Austin on which to erect a permanent building. The new center opened in 1995. In 1998, it was renamed the Lady Bird Johnson Wildflower Center. Now, with 279 acres, more than 700 plant species on display, and a fully developed education program for children and adults, the Wildflower Center's influence is strong across the Nation.

With its mission of increasing the sustainable use and conservation of native wildflowers, plants and landscapes, the center works to teach everyone how these plants conserve water, minimize the use of fertilizers and insecticides that pollute the atmosphere and convey a unique sense of place.

"It is not just one organization, one location," said Mrs. Johnson's daughter, Luci Baines Johnson. "It is a philosophy that will endure long after my mother is not here, and I think there is no legacy she would more treasure than to have helped people recognize the value in preserving and promoting our native land."

In an article in the Organization of American Historians' *Magazine of History*, historian Rita G. Koman said, "LADY BIRD JOHNSON's legacy was to legitimize environmental issues as a national priority. The attitudes and policies she advanced have shaped the conservation and preservation policies of the environmental movement since then."

Lewis L. Gould, University of Texas professor and author of "LADY BIRD JOHNSON and the Environmental Movement," wrote in his preface:

> If a man in the 1960s had been involved with an environmental movement such as highway beautification, had changed the appearance of a major American city, had addressed the problems of black inner-city youth and had campaigned tirelessly to enhance national concern about natural beauty, no doubts would be raised that he was worthy of biographical and scholarly scrutiny. LADY BIRD JOHNSON's accomplishments [served] as a catalyst for environmental ideas during the 1960s and thereafter entitle her to an evaluation of what she tried to do and what she achieved.

LADY BIRD JOHNSON was honored by President Ford by being named to the Advisory Council to the American Revolution Bicentennial Administration. In 1977, President Jimmy Carter appointed Mrs. JOHNSON to the President's Commission on White House Fellowships. In 1966 she received the George Foster Peabody Award for the television program, "A Visit to Washington with Mrs. LYNDON B. JOHNSON on Behalf of a More Beautiful America."

Mrs. JOHNSON was awarded the Medal of Freedom by President Gerald Ford in 1977, and the Congressional Gold Medal in 1988.

Her more than 50 awards include the Eleanor Roosevelt Golden Candlestick Award, Women's National Press Club, 1968; Conservation Service Award, Department of the Interior, 1974; American Legion Distinguished Award, 1975; *Ladies Home Journal* "Woman of the Year" Award for Quality of Life, 1975; Texas Women's Hall of Fame, 1984; National Achievement Award, American Horticultural Society, 1984; Wildflowers Across America Award of the

Year, Garden Writers Association, 1984; Texan of the Year Award, State of Texas, 1985; and the Daughters of the American Revolution Medal of Honor, 2003.

LADY BIRD JOHNSON's more than 15 honorary degrees include a doctor of letters in 1964 from the University of Texas, Austin, TX; doctor of law in 1964 from Texas Woman's University, Denton, TX; a doctor of public service in 1986 from George Washington University; and a doctor of humane letters in 1990 from Johns Hopkins University.

Claudia "Lady Bird" Taylor in graduation cap and gown.

Austin Statesman

Lady Bird Johnson with movie camera.

Lyndon B. Johnson and Lady Bird Johnson posing in front of the
Capitol.

Lady Bird Johnson planting a cherry tree.

Yoichi Okamoto

Lady Bird Johnson, President Lyndon B. Johnson, and Yuki sitting near the Pedernales River.

Robert Knudsen

Lady Bird Johnson visits classroom for Project Head Start.

LBJ Library photo by Robert Knudsen

Portrait of Lady Bird Johnson in the White House, May 8, 1968.

Frank Wolfe

Left to right: Lyndon Nugent, Jennifer Robb, Nicole Nugent, Claudia Nugent, Lady Bird Johnson, Lucinda Robb, Rebekah Nugent,
Catherine Robb.

THE HOLY EUCHARIST: RITE TWO

THE LITURGY
FOR THE PROCLAMATION
OF THE
WORD OF GOD
AND CELEBRATION OF THE
HOLY COMMUNION
IN THANKSGIVING FOR THE LIFE OF
LADY BIRD JOHNSON

THE WORD OF GOD

HYMN: MORNING HAS BROKEN
Bunessan

>Morning has broken like the first morning,
>blackbird has spoken like the first bird.
>Praise for the singing! Praise for the morning!
>Praise for them springing, fresh from the Word!
>
>Sweet the rain's new fall sunlit from heaven,
>like the first dewfall on the first grass.
>Praise for the sweetness of the wet garden,
>sprung in completeness, where his feet pass.
>
>Mine is the sunlight! Mine is the morning,
>born of the one light Eden saw play!
>Praise with elation, praise every morning,
>God's recreation of the new day!

The people standing, the Celebrant says

Celebrant
Alleluia. Christ is risen.

People
The Lord is risen indeed. Alleluia.

The Celebrant says
Almighty God, to you all hearts are open, all desires known, and from you no secrets are hid: Cleanse the thoughts of our hearts by the inspiration of your Holy Spirit, that we may perfectly love you, and worthily magnify your holy Name; through Christ our Lord. Amen.

THE COLLECT OF THE DAY

The Celebrant says to the people
The Lord be with you.

People
And also with you.

Celebrant
Let us pray.

Almighty God, we remember before you today your faithful servant CLAUDIA; and we pray that, having opened to her the gates of larger life, you will receive her more and more into your joyful service, that, with all who have faithfully served you in the past, she may share in the eternal victory of Jesus

Christ our Lord; who lives and reigns with you, in the unity of the Holy Spirit, one God, for ever and ever. Amen.

THE LESSONS

The people sit.

READING: ISAIAH 61:1–3

READING: PHILIPPIANS 4:4–9

The people stand and say together Psalm 23

PSALM: PSALM 23

The LORD is my shepherd; I shall not be in want.

He makes me lie down in green pastures and leads me beside still waters.

He revives my soul and guides me along right pathways for his Name's sake.

Though I walk through the valley of the shadow of death, I shall fear no evil;
for you are with me;
your rod and your staff, they comfort me.

You spread a table before me in the presence of those who trouble me;
you have anointed my head with oil,
and my cup is running over.

Surely your goodness and mercy shall follow me all the days of my life,
and I will dwell in the house of the LORD for ever.

Then, all standing, the Priest reads the Gospel, first saying

The Holy Gospel of our Lord Jesus Christ according to Matthew 5:1–12

People

Glory to you, Lord Christ.

After the Gospel, the Reader says

The Gospel of the Lord.

People

Praise to you, Lord Christ.

The people sit.

THE HOMILY

The people stand.

THE PRAYERS OF THE PEOPLE

Dear Friends: It was our Lord Jesus himself who said, "Come to me, all you who labor and are burdened, and I will give you rest."

Let us pray, then, for our beloved CLAUDIA, that she may rest from her labors, and enter into the light of God's eternal sabbath rest.

Receive, O Lord, your servant, for she returns to you.

Into your hands, O Lord, we commend our sister CLAUDIA.

Wash her in the holy font of everlasting life, and clothe her in his heavenly wedding garment.

Into your hands, O Lord, we commend our sister CLAUDIA.

May she hear your words of invitation, "Come, you blessed of my Father."

Into your hands, O Lord, we commend our sister CLAUDIA.

May she gaze upon you, Lord, face to face, and taste the blessedness of perfect rest.

Into your hands, O Lord, we commend our sister CLAUDIA.

May angels surround her, and saints welcome her in peace.

Into your hands, O Lord, we commend our sister CLAUDIA.

The Celebrant concludes

Almighty God, our Father in heaven, before whom live all who die in the Lord: Receive our beloved CLAUDIA into the courts of your heavenly dwelling place. Let her heart and soul now ring out in joy to you, O Lord, the living God, and the God of those who live. This we ask through Christ our Lord. Amen.

HYMN: IN CHRIST THERE IS NO EAST OR WEST
McKee, Afro-American spiritual

In Christ there is no East or West,
in him no South or North,
but one great fellowship of love,
throughout the whole wide world.

Join hands, disciples of the faith,

what e'er your race may be!
Who serves my Father as his child
is surely kin to me.

In Christ now meet both East and West,
in him meet South and North,
all Christly souls are one in him,
throughout the whole wide earth.

THE HOLY COMMUNION

The people remain standing. The Celebrant faces them and says

Celebrant
The Lord be with you.

People
And also with you.

Celebrant
Lift up your hearts.

People
We lift them to the Lord.

Celebrant
Let us give thanks to the Lord our God.

People
It is right to give him thanks and praise.

Then the Celebrant proceeds
It is right, and a good and joyful thing, always and everywhere to give thanks to you, Father Almighty, Creator of heaven and earth, through Jesus Christ our Lord; who rose victorious from the dead, and comforts us with the blessed hope of everlasting life. For to your faithful people, O Lord, life is changed, not ended; and when our mortal body lies in death, there is prepared for us a dwelling place eternal in the heavens.

Therefore we praise you, joining our voices with Angels and Archangels and with all the company of heaven, who for ever sing this hymn to proclaim the glory of your Name:

Celebrant and People
Holy, holy, holy Lord, God of power and might,
heaven and earth are full of your glory.

Hosanna in the highest.

Blessed is he who comes in the name of the Lord.

Hosanna in the highest.

Then the Celebrant continues

We give thanks to you, O God, for the goodness and love which you have made known to us in creation; in the calling of Israel to be your people; in your Word spoken through the prophets; and above all in the Word made flesh, Jesus, your Son. For in these last days you sent him to be incarnate from the Virgin Mary, to be the Savior and Redeemer of the world. In him, you have delivered us from evil, and made us worthy to stand before you. In him, you have brought us out of error into truth, out of sin into righteousness, out of death into life.

On the night before he died for us, our Lord Jesus Christ took bread; and when he had given thanks to you, he broke it, and gave it to his disciples, and said, "Take, eat: This is my Body, which is given for you. Do this for the remembrance of me."

After supper he took the cup of wine; and when he had given thanks, he gave it to them, and said, "Drink this, all of you: This is my Blood of the new Covenant, which is shed for you and for many for the forgiveness of sins. Whenever you drink it, do this for the remembrance of me."

Therefore, according to his command, O Father,

Celebrant and People

We remember his death,
We proclaim his resurrection,
We await his coming in glory;

The Celebrant continues

And we offer our sacrifice of praise and thanksgiving to you, O Lord of all; presenting to you, from your creation, this bread and this wine.

We pray you, gracious God, to send your Holy Spirit upon these gifts that they may be the Sacrament of the Body of Christ and his Blood of the new Covenant. Unite us to your Son in his sacrifice, that we may be acceptable through him, being sanctified by the Holy Spirit. In the fullness of time, put all things in subjection under your Christ, and bring us to that heavenly country where, with CLAUDIA TAYLOR JOHNSON and all your saints, we may enter the everlasting heritage of your sons and daughters; through Jesus Christ our Lord, the first-born of all creation, the head of the Church, and the author of our salvation.

By him, and with him, and in him, in the unity of the Holy Spirit all honor and glory is yours, Almighty Father, now and for ever. Amen.

And now, as our Savior
Christ has taught us,
we are bold to say,

People and Celebrant
Our Father, who art in heaven,
Hallowed be thy Name,
Thy kingdom come,
Thy will be done,
On earth as it is in heaven.
Give us this day our daily bread.
And forgive us our trespasses,
As we forgive those who trespass against us.
And lead us not into temptation,
But deliver us from evil.
For thine is the kingdom,
And the power, and the glory,
For ever and ever.
Amen.

THE BREAKING OF THE BREAD

The Celebrant breaks the consecrated Bread.
A period of silence is kept.
Then the Celebrant says
Alleluia. Christ our Passover is sacrificed for us;

People
Therefore let us keep the feast. Alleluia.

Facing the people, the Celebrant says the following Invitation
The Gifts of God for the People of God.

After Communion, the Celebrant says
Let us pray together:

Almighty God, we thank you that in your great love you have fed us with the spiritual food and drink of the Body and Blood of your Son Jesus Christ, and have given us a foretaste of your heavenly banquet. Grant that this Sacrament may be to us a comfort in affliction, and a pledge of our inheritance in that kingdom where there is no death, neither sorrow nor crying, but the fullness of joy with all your saints; through Jesus Christ our Savior. Amen.

The people stand.

THE PEACE

Celebrant
    The peace of the Lord be always with you.

People
    And also with you.

Then the Ministers and People may greet one another in the name of the Lord.

DISMISSAL

In Celebration of the Life of Lady Bird Johnson
1912 – 2007

"As I look back on those five years of turmoil and achievement, of triumph and pain, I feel amazement that it happened to me, and gratitude that I had the opportunity to live them, and strongest of all—out of all the trips that I made and all the people that I met— a deep, roaring faith in and love for this country."

Lady Bird Johnson
A White House Diary, 1970

Dear Loved Ones,

Thank you for sharing in the celebration of our mother's, grandmother's, and great-grandmother's life.

We know that Mother had many families. She had national, political, business, beautification, university, library, and most especially, wildflower families.

For ninety-four years, she mothered them all selflessly, giving the first fruits of her powerful intellect, gentle understanding, insatiable curiosity, benevolent spirit, and time.

We recognize that, in many ways, you thought of her as your mother, too.

We know you join us in mourning her loss, giving thanks for her life well lived, and rejoicing that her suffering in recent years has been replaced by the joy of salvation.

Mother believed in all her families and made each feel she loved them best. We pray that our service to her families may be a credit to her example, for that is the just tribute to a mother's love.

We love you for loving her,

Lynda and Chuck Robb
Luci Baines Johnson and Ian Turpin
Lyndon and Nicole Nugent
Lucinda Robb and Lars Florio
Nicole and Brent Covert
Catherine Lewis Robb
Rebekah and Jeremy McIntosh
Claudia and Steven Brod
Jennifer Robb
Tatum Rebekah and Taylor Baines Nugent
Johnson and Claudia Covert
Eloise, Tucker, and Luci Bella McIntosh
Sophia Baines and Isabella Taylor Brod
Madeline Taylor Florio

Lady Bird Johnson touring the Giant Redwoods in Eureka, CA, on
November 25, 1968.

IN TRIBUTE

Today we say our personal farewells to LADY BIRD JOHNSON for her friendship and her abiding love of the land for all to enjoy. She exemplified what conscientious people must strive to do: make a difference.

Today where wildflowers grow free and landscapes are not hidden, we are grateful she was the crucial catalyst, accomplishing this with a gentle hand and tender voice as she led a rebellion against ugliness. She rallied not only powerful allies, but millions of unknown followers to the cause of the environment's best and did it with her own strong words:

"Ugliness is so grim. A little beauty, something that is lovely, can create harmony that will lessen tensions. The time is ripe—the time is now—to take advantage of this yeasty, bubbling desire to beautify our cities and our countryside."

It lifted the stature of those environmentalists who had been struggling at city halls and state legislatures. As a result of her courageous voice and national following, she put the environment on the agenda of every person in public life—where it remains.

Politics was not her choice for a life, but she gave her loyalty to its purposes and did it with grace, eloquence, and humor. Realistic always, she said, "One of the earmarks of campaigning is total confusion ... it means early sun-ups and cold pancakes."

She was always there, not just for her husband and son-in-law, but in later years, for family and friends who were swept into public life by the Great Society and her abiding faith "that the path of mankind is always upward." She wrote checks and she gave open support.

Her style was natural with unassuming warmth as refreshing as the sweet scent of the East Texas piney woods where she grew up pretty much alone, after her mother's death at age five. She recalled playing around the gnarled old roots of the cypress trees on Caddo Lake and delighting in finding the first violets of spring. Her commitment to the cause of leaving nature's beauty unmolested became a movement.

Her love for her husband withstood all attacks. "He is an exciting man to live with, and an exhausting man to keep up with, and one who has taught me that to put all the heart and skill and brains you have into trying to make your government work a little bit better, can be a wonderful life for a man—and his wife." She translated his causes for Head Start, the Job Corps, and the War on Poverty with trips throughout the country, taking reporters along "to help the public look, see, and hopefully act."

When she moved into the White House, she told reporters, "I have moved on stage to a part I never rehearsed."

There was no need for one.

Liz Carpenter

ORDER OF SERVICE

PRELUDE: BRASS ENSEMBLE
Combined Choirs of Ebenezer Baptist Church and Huston-Tillotson University

OPENING SENTENCE: JOHN 14:1–3
Let not your hearts be troubled; believe in God, believe also in me. In my Father's house are many rooms; if it were not so, would I have told you that I go to prepare a place for you? And when I go and prepare a place for you, I will come again and will take you to myself, that where I am you may be also.

Please stand as the family is seated and remain standing for the opening hymn.

OPENING HYMN: HYMN TO JOY
Choir and Congregation
Joyful, joyful, we adore thee,
God of glory, Lord of love;
Hearts unfold like flowers before thee,
Praising thee, their sun above.
Melt the clouds of sin and sadness;
Drive the dark of doubt away;
Giver of immortal gladness,
Fill us with the light of day.

All thy works with joy surround thee,
Earth and heaven reflect thy rays,
Stars and angels sing around thee,
Center of unbroken praise:
Field and forest, vale and mountain,
Blooming meadow, flashing sea,
Chanting bird and flowing fountain,
Call us to rejoice in thee.

Thou art giving and forgiving,
Ever blessing, ever blest,
Well-spring of the joy of living,
Ocean-depth of happy rest!
Thou our Father, Christ our Brother:
All who live in love are thine;
Teach us how to love each other,
Lift us to the joy divine.

Amen.

COLLECT
The Reverend Dean Pratt

O God of grace and glory, we remember before you this day our sister CLAUDIA. We thank you for giving her to us, her family and friends, to know and to love as a companion on our earthly pilgrimage. In your boundless compassion, console us who mourn. Give us faith to see in death the gate of eternal life, so that in quiet confidence we may continue our course on earth, until, by your call, we are reunited with those who have gone before; through Jesus Christ our Lord. Amen.

Please sit

FIRST READING: WISDOM 3:1–3; DANIEL 12:3
Claudia Taylor Brod

The souls of the righteous are in the hand of God, and no torment will ever touch them. In the eyes of the foolish they seemed to have died, and their departure was thought to be a disaster, and their going from us to be their destruction; but they are at peace. Those who trust in him will understand truth, and the faithful will abide with him in love, because grace and mercy are upon his holy ones, and he watches over his elect. Those who are wise shall shine like the brightness of the sky, and those who lead many to righteousness, like the stars forever and ever.

PSALM: PSALM 46
Rebekah Johnson Nugent McIntosh

God is our hope and strength,*
a very present help in trouble.

Therefore will we not fear, though the earth be moved,*
and though the hills be carried into the midst of the sea;

Though the waters thereof rage and swell,*
and though the mountains shake at the tempest of the same.

There is a river, the streams whereof make glad the city of God,*
the holy place of the tabernacle of the Most High.

God is in the midst of her,
therefore shall she not be removed;*
God shall help her, and that right early.

Be still then, and know that I am God;*
I will be exalted among the nations,
and I will be exalted in the earth.

The Lord of hosts is with us;*
the God of Jacob is our refuge.

SECOND READING: ROMANS 8:14–19; 34–35; 37–39
Jennifer Robb

Who will separate us from the love of Christ? Will hardship, or distress, or persecution, or famine, or nakedness, or peril, or sword? No, in all these things we are more than conquerors through him who loved us. For I am convinced that neither, death, nor life, nor angels, nor rulers, nor things present, nor things to come, nor powers, nor height, nor depth, nor anything else in all creation, will be able to separate us from the love of God in Jesus Christ our Lord.

REMEMBERING
Tom Johnson
Harry Middleton

Please stand

HYMN: FOR THE BEAUTY OF THE EARTH
Choir and Congregation

For the beauty of the earth,
For the beauty of the skies,
For the love which from our birth
Over and around us lies,

Lord of all, to thee we raise
This our hymn of grateful praise.

For the beauty of each hour
Of the day and of the night,
Hill and vale, and tree and flower,
Sun and moon, and stars of light,

Refrain

For the joy of human love,
Brother, sister, parent, child,
Friends on earth, and friends above,
For all gentle thoughts and mild,

Refrain

Amen.

GOSPEL: MATTHEW 6:25–33
The Reverend Patsy Chaney

"Therefore I tell you, do not worry about your life, what you will eat or what you will drink, or about your body, what you will wear. Is not life more than food, and the body more than clothing? Look at the birds of the air; they neither sow nor reap nor gather into barns, and yet your heavenly Father feeds them. Are you not of more value than they? And can any of you by worrying add a single hour to your span of life? And why do you worry about clothing? Consider the lilies of the field, how they grow; they neither toil nor spin, yet I tell you, even Solomon in all his glory was not clothed like one of these. But if God so clothes the grass of the field, which is alive today and tomorrow is thrown into the oven, will he not much more clothe you—you of little faith? Therefore do not worry, saying, 'What will we eat?' or 'What will we drink?' or 'What will we wear?' For it is the Gentiles who strive for all these things; and indeed your heavenly Father knows that you need all these things. But strive first for the kingdom of God and his righteousness, and all these things will be given to you as well."

Please sit

HOMILY
Bill Moyers

Please stand

HYMN: IN THE GARDEN
Choir and Congregation

I come to the garden alone,
While the dew is still on the roses:
And the voice I hear, falling on my ear,
The Son of God discloses.

And He walks with me, and He talks with me,
And He tells me I am His own;
And the joy we share as we tarry there,
None other has ever known.

He speaks, and the sound of His voice
Is so sweet the birds hush their singing,
And the melody that He gave to me,
Within my heart is ringing.

Refrain

FAMILY TRIBUTE
    Nicole Covert
    Lucinda Robb
    Catherine Lewis Robb
    Lynda Robb
    Luci Baines Johnson

Please stand

THE LORD'S PRAYER
In unison
    Our Father, who art in heaven,
    Hallowed be thy Name,
    Thy kingdom come,
    Thy will be done,
    On earth as it is in heaven.
    Give us this day our daily bread.
    And forgive us our trespasses,
    As we forgive those who trespass against us.
    And lead us not into temptation,
    But deliver us from evil.
    For thine is the kingdom,
    And the power, and the glory,
    For ever and ever.
    Amen.

COMMENDATION
The Right Reverend John McCarthy
    Into your hands, O merciful Savior, we commend your servant
    CLAUDIA. Acknowledge, we humbly beseech you, a sheep of
    your own fold, a lamb of your own flock, a sinner of your own
    redeeming. Receive her into the arms of your mercy, into the
    blessed rest of everlasting peace, and into the glorious com-
    pany of the saints in light. Amen.

BENEDICTION
    And now may the blessing of the Lord rest and remain upon
    all his people, in every land, of every tongue. The Lord meet
    in mercy all that seek him. The Lord comfort all that suffer
    and mourn. The Lord hasten his kingdom, and give you and
    all his people peace forevermore. Amen.

HYMN: AMERICA THE BEAUTIFUL
Choir and Congregation
    O beautiful for spacious skies,

For amber waves of grain,
For purple mountain majesties
Above the fruited plain!
America! America!
God shed His grace on thee,
And crown thy good with brotherhood
From sea to shining sea!

O beautiful for patriot dream
That sees beyond the years
Thine alabaster cities gleam
Undimmed by human tears.
America! America!
God shed his grace on thee,
And crown thy good with brotherhood
From sea to shining sea.

MUSICAL TRIBUTE: THE EYES OF TEXAS
Band and Congregation, University of Texas Longhorn Band
The Eyes of Texas are upon you,
All the livelong day.
The Eyes of Texas are upon you,
You cannot get away.
Do not think you can escape them,
From night 'til early in the morn.
The Eyes of Texas are upon you,
'Til Gabriel blows his horn.

RECESSIONAL
Instrumental

DISMISSAL

Lyndon Nugent will deliver the Family Tribute at the private burial service. That service will be conducted by The Reverend Richard Elwood.

Holy Communion in thanksgiving for the life of Lady Bird Johnson was celebrated at the Lady Bird Johnson Wildflower Center, under the direction of The Reverend Stephen Kinney.

The private burial will be at The Johnson Family Cemetery on the banks of the Pedernales River.

Tom Johnson

Heaven is even a more beautiful place today because LADY BIRD JOHNSON is there.

A new angel has entered the Pearly Gates, and there now are Texas bluebonnets planted along those streets of gold.

As heartbreaking as it is to lose Mrs. JOHNSON here on earth, it is comforting to know that she once again can see the wonders of another world, that she again can read the books she loved so dearly, that she is once again reunited with her man for rides together around the Great Ranch in the Sky.

I can imagine her saying to LBJ, "Now, Lyndon, didn't our Lynda and Luci and their children and grandchildren turn out just wonderfully!"

And, I can imagine LBJ responding: "Oh, yes, they did. I give all of them 'A plus.'"

In another conversation sure to take place soon, President JOHNSON will say:

"Even though you and Harry Middleton opened those sealed White House tape recordings about 40 years earlier than I had directed, it was another wise decision by you. They actually seem to have helped my reputation."

And, indeed—they have.

President JOHNSON often said, "Texans care about you when you are sick, and they come to your funeral when you die."

Well, today not just Texans but people across the Nation mourn the loss of LADY BIRD JOHNSON.

Gathered here are so many of those who loved her most of all:

Lynda and Luci and their families. She took such incredible pride in you. And you have cared for her with such magnificent devotion and love.

The LBJ Ranch staff and office staff provided such loyalty to her throughout her lifetime. It was a labor of love, and she knew it.

Her Secret Service agents who always protected her and watched over her with special thoughtfulness and respect. She thought of you as her friends, a part of her expanded family.

Her White House staffs, especially Liz Carpenter and Bess Abel, and all those who supported her while she was First Lady.

Her beautification team, those who joined her efforts in the White House and those who brought to life the splendid National Wildflower Center here in Austin.

Her last wish—to unite the Wildflower Center with her beloved University of Texas—became a reality thanks to so many of you here today.

And her dearest personal friends and travel partners.

Wasn't she just the best host in Acapulco, at Martha's Vineyard, in Italy, in France, in Greece, in Egypt? I bet she and Bob Waldron already are planning their next heavenly trip.

Each and every one of us has been touched in some way by the magic that was LADY BIRD.

Who can ever see another field of wildflowers without thinking of her?

Who can forget all our conversations with her? She so loved good conversations, especially to hear about our children, and our grandchildren, about what good books we had read, and what interesting trips we had made.

To hear her talk always was an unforgettable experience. She chose each word carefully. Her words of wisdom will remain with me throughout my lifetime.

You have heard this before, but I think it deserves repeating:

I asked her once, "Mrs. J., what is the favorite gift of all those you have received in your lifetime?"

She replied: "Tom, the best gift you can give another person is the gift of a good memory."

Well, Mrs. J., you gave us all so many beautiful memories.

Whenever Edwina and I see a wildflower, we will have our wonderful memories of you.

Whenever we take a trip, we will have our splendid memories of our magnificent trips with you.

Whenever we read a great book, we will recall your great love of reading and our discussions of those books with you.

Mrs. J, you enriched our lives, and the lives of millions of people everywhere.

We have lost and heaven has gained—one of the best the world contained.

Goodbye, Mrs. J., we will be seeing you again.

Harry Middleton

A sentimental ballad from days long gone plays in my mind: "I'll Be Seeing You."

The lyrics of that song of half a century ago tell of carousels and sidewalk cafes and wishing wells. The images of LADY BIRD it conjures up are of a different order. They are of color and achievement and fulfillment. If the song had been written with her in mind, it would go more along these lines:

I'll be seeing you in every burst of roadside bloom ...
In every Head Start schoolhouse room ...

I'll be seeing her—we all will—whenever we chance upon a cof-
fee-can geranium sitting on a window sill, when we watch strollers
on the trail around Town Lake, whenever, indeed, we know the return of spring. She created, and left for us all, memories to garnish
a lifetime. All kinds of memories. She was so much to so many.
"Some people," John Gardner said of her, "make the world a special
place just by being the kind of people they are. That's LADY BIRD."

And beyond the well-known qualities that make the world a better place were others that may not have been counted in that cal-
culus, but nonetheless contributed immeasurable to the pleasure of
many of us.

A quality that I want to celebrate today, before she is left to history, is one that will not be found in her official biography, but is
an essential part of the memory I carry. She was fun, just a whale
of a lot of fun to be with. She had a delicious sense of humor, sometimes slightly mischievous, not always in keeping with her image.

It was my good fortune to spend part of every summer with her
on Martha's Vineyard. Our first visit there was some 30 years ago.
It was only for a week, but a week with a tiring schedule, entirely
packed with activities. Each night was the occasion for at least two,
sometimes three, festive events. One evening, halfway through the
week, as we sped from a cocktail party to a dinner, she said: "I
don't know why I am doing this." Then, remember, this was 30
years ago, and the language and slogans of the 1960s were still
part of our on-going experience, she said: "Well, I do know. It's because I didn't say 'HELL NO, I WON'T GO!'"

Then there was the time we were in New York having a breakfast meeting in the dining room of the Plaza Hotel. The members
of a rock singing group, calling themselves the Village People were
seated there, too, all in full costume, one as a construction worker,
another as a policeman, another as an Indian. Recognizing Mrs.
JOHNSON, the leader came over, introduced the group, proclaimed
his admiration, and asked if she would have her picture taken with
them. Ever gracious, she of course agreed.

Afterward, she asked and was told who they were. She smiled.
"Well," she said, "I wonder if we just made the cover of their next
album."

It was an element, a fascinating element, of her many-splendored
personality, as her forbearance was, and her keen intelligence, and
the indomitable spirit of her final days.

In all her varieties, she brought a special charm into our world,
a special mix of grace and steel, of wit and wisdom, a special blend
of so many causes, so many contributions, so many things to value.

"Thank you for showing us the beauty around us," a woman
wrote her recently. On the anniversary of Head Start, the program

to open educational opportunities to poor children, which she launched as National Chairman, many wrote to tell her how that program had changed their lives.

They wrote to her on a myriad of issues over the years.

"She lit a fire in this country that has never gone out," a colleague of her White House days said of her.

It has never gone out, and it won't. It glows in places and hearts without number.

It glows in mine. And it beats with the rhythm of a time when the world was younger, when we shared the great adventure of building a historic institution to preserve a noble legacy.

I'll be seeing her in all the places of beauty she created and touched. I'll remember her always for her courage and the strength of her support. And I'll think of her and hear her voice in all the memories of joy and laughter she brought to my life.

Bill Moyers, PBS journalist, Special Assistant to President Lyndon Johnson 1963–1967

It is unthinkable to me that LADY BIRD is gone.

She was so much a part of the landscape, so much a part of our lives and our times, so much a part of our country for so long that I began to imagine her with us always. Now, although the fields of purple, orange, and blue will long evoke her gifts to us, that vibrant presence has departed, and we are left to mourn our loss of her even as we celebrate her life.

Some people arriving earlier today were asked, "Are you sitting with the family?" I looked around at this throng and said to myself, "Everyone here is sitting with the family. That's how she would treat us. All of us."

When I arrived in Washington in 1954 to work in the LBJ mailroom between my sophomore and junior years, I didn't know a single person in town, not even the Johnsons, whom I only met that first week. She soon recognized that weekends were especially lonesome for me, and she called one day to ask me over for Sunday brunch.

I had never even heard of Sunday brunch, much less been to one; for all I knew, it was an Episcopalian sacrament. When I arrived at 30th Place the family was there, the little girls, LADY BIRD and himself. But so were Richard Russell and Sam Rayburn and J. Edgar Hoover. They didn't look like Episcopal priests to me. They were sitting around the smallish room reading the newspaper, except for LBJ, who was on the phone. If this is their idea of a sacrament, I thought, I'll just stay a Baptist. But Mrs. JOHNSON knew something about the bachelors she had invited there, including the kid fresh up from her native East Texas. On a Sunday morning they needed a family, and she had offered us communion at her table. In a way, it was a sacrament.

It was also very good politics. She told me something that summer that would make a difference in my life. She was shy, and in the presence of powerful men, she usually kept her counsel. Sensing that I was shy, too, and aware I had no experience to enforce any opinions, she said: "Don't worry. If you are unsure of what to say, just ask questions, and I promise you that when they leave, they will think you were the smartest one in the room, just for listening to them. Word will get around," she said.

She knew the ways of the world, and how they could be made to work for you, even when you didn't fully understand what was going on. She told me once, years later, that she didn't even understand everything about the man she married, nor did she want to, she said, as long as he needed her.

Oh, he needed her, all right. You know the famous incident. Once, trying to locate her in a crowded room, he growled aloud: "Where's LADY BIRD?" And she replied: "Right behind you, darling, where I've always been."

"Whoever loves, believes the impossible," Elizabeth Browning wrote. LADY BIRD truly loved this man she often found impossible. "I'm no more bewildered by Lyndon than he is bewildered by himself," she once told me.

Like everyone he loved, she often found herself in the path of his Vesuvian eruptions. During the campaign of 1960 I slept in the bed in their basement when we returned from the road for sessions of the Senate. She knew I was lonesome for Judith and our 6-month-old son who were back in Texas. She would often come down the two flights of stairs to ask if I was doing all right. One night the Senator and I got home even later than usual. And he brought with him some unresolved dispute from the Senate Cloakroom. At midnight I could still hear him upstairs, carrying on as if he were about to purge the Democratic caucus. Pretty soon I heard her footsteps on the stairs and I called out: "Mrs. JOHNSON, you don't need to check up on me. I'm all right." And she called back, "Well, I was coming down to tell you I'm all right, too."

She seemed to grow calmer as the world around her became more furious.

Thunderstorms struck in her life so often you had to wonder why the gods on Olympus kept testing her. She lost her mother in an accident when she was 5. She was two cars behind JFK in Dallas. She was in the White House when Martin Luther King was shot and Washington burned. She grieved for the family of Robert Kennedy, and for the lives lost in Vietnam.

Early in the White House, a well-meaning editor up from Texas said, "You poor thing, having to follow Jackie Kennedy." Mrs. JOHNSON's mouth dropped open in amazed disbelief. And she said, "Oh, no, don't pity me. Weep for Mrs. Kennedy. She lost her husband. I still have my Lyndon."

She aimed for the consolation and comfort of others. It was not only her talent at negotiating the civil war raging in his nature. It was not just the way she remained unconscripted by the factions into which family, friends, and advisers inevitably divide around a powerful figure. She did her best to keep open all the roads to reconciliation.

Like her beloved flowers in the field, she was a woman of many hues. A strong manager, a canny investor, a shrewd judge of people, friend and foe, and she never confused the two. Deliberate in coming to judgment, she was sure in conclusion.

But let me speak especially of the one quality that most captured my admiration and affection, her courage.

It is the fall of 1960. We're in Dallas, where neither Kennedy nor Johnson are local heroes. We start across the street from the Adolphus to the Baker Hotel. The reactionary Congressman from Dallas has organized a demonstration of women, pretty women, in costumes of red, white, and blue, waving little American flags above their cowboy hats. At first I take them to be cheerleaders having a good time. But suddenly they are an angry mob, snarling, salivating, spitting.

A roar, a primal terrifying roar swells around us, my first experience with collective hate roused to a fever pitch. I'm right behind the Johnsons. She's taken his arm and as she turns left and right, nodding to the mob, I can see she is smiling. And I see in the eyes of some of those women a confusion, what I take to be their realization that this is them at their most uncivil, confronting a woman who is the triumph of civility. So help me, her very demeanor creates a small zone of grace in the midst of that tumultuous throng. And they move back a little, and again a little, Mrs. JOHNSON continuing to nod and smile, until we're inside the Baker and upstairs in the suite.

Now LBJ is smiling, he knows that Texas was up for grabs until this moment, and the backlash will decide it for us. But Mrs. JOHNSON has pulled back the curtains and is looking down that street as the mob disperses. She has seen a dark and disturbing omen. Still holding the curtain back, as if she were peering into the future, she says, "Things will never be the same again."

Now it is 1964. The disinherited descendants of slavery, still denied their rights as citizens after a century of segregation, have resolved to claim for themselves the American promise of life, liberty, and the pursuit of happiness. President Johnson has thrown the full power of his office to their side. He has just signed the Civil Rights Acts of 1964, the greatest single sword of justice raised for equality since the Emancipation Proclamation. A few weeks later, both Johnsons plunge into his campaign for election in his own right. After that historic legislation he has more or less given up on the South, but she will not. These were her people, here were her roots. And she is not ready to sever them. So she sets out on a whistle-stop journey of nearly 1700 miles through the heart of her past. She is on her own now, campaigning independently, across the Mason-Dixon line past the buckle of the Bible Belt all the way down to the Port of New Orleans. I cannot all these years later do justice to what she faced: The boos, the jeers, the hecklers, the crude signs and cruder gestures, the insults and the threats. This is the land still ruled by Jim Crow and John Birch, who control the law with the cross and enforce it with the club. It is 1964, and bathroom signs still read: "White Ladies" and "Colored Women."

In Richmond, she is greeted with signs that read: "Fly away, LADY BIRD." In Charleston, "Blackbird Go Home." Children planted in the front row hold up signs practically in her face: "Johnson is a Nigger Lover." In Savannah they curse her daughter. The air has become so menacing we run a separate engine 15 minutes ahead of her in case of a bomb. She later said, "People were concerned for me, but I was concerned for the engineer in the train out in front; he was in far greater danger." Rumors spread of snipers, and in the panhandle of Florida the threats are so ominous the FBI orders a yard-by-yard sweep of a 7-mile bridge that her train would cross.

She never flinches. Up to 40 times a day from the platform of the caboose she will speak, sometimes raising a single white-gloved hand to punctuate her words, always the lady. When the insults grew so raucous in South Carolina, she tells the crowd the ugly words were coming "not from the good people of South Carolina but from the state of confusion." In Columbia she answers hecklers with what one observer called "a maternal bark." And she says, "This is a country of many viewpoints. I respect your right to express your own. Now is my turn to express mine."

An advance man called me back at the White House from the pay phone at a local train depot. He was choking back the tears. "As long as I live," he said, in a voice breaking with emotion, "I will thank God I was here today, so that I can tell my children that I saw the difference courage makes."

Yes, she planted flowers, and wanted and worked for highways and parks and vistas that opened us to the Technicolor splendors of our world. Walk this weekend among the paths and trails and flowers and see the beauty she loved. But as you do, remember, she also loved democracy, and saw a beauty in it, rough though the ground may be, hard and stony, as tangled and as threatened with blight as nature itself. And remember that this shy little girl from Karnack, TX, with eyes as wistful as cypress and manners as soft as the whispering pine, grew up to show us how to cultivate the beauty in democracy: The voice raised against the mob, the courage to overcome fear with convictions as true as steel. CLAUDIA ALTA TAYLOR, LADY BIRD JOHNSON, served the beauty in nature and the beauty in us, and right down to the end of her long and bountiful life, she inspired us to serve them, too.

Nicole Covert

My name is Nicole Nugent Covert and I am the third grandchild of CLAUDIA ALTA TAYLOR JOHNSON, aka LADY BIRD JOHNSON, First Lady, Wildflower Lady but known to her family as just Nini. My role here today is to share with you a little insight on one of the many titles that my grandmother had. Yes, it is true that she served our country lovingly and dutifully as First Lady. It is also true that she was devoted to her precious daughters, Lynda and Luci. The dedication and loyalty that ran and will continue to run amongst the three of them are such strong ones that I too can only hope that I share that same experience with my mother, siblings, and children.

I would like to think that her favorite role was that of grand-mother. There will never be another Nini. In my youth there were times that we were to be seen and not heard. In my childhood there was a children's table—I might also add that it was in the kitchen at the ranch—far enough away from the dining room so that the grown ups wouldn't be disturbed. In my youth, Christmas at the ranch was the biggest deal—still is—even to the grown ups. In my youth, there were trips to exotic countries and discoveries of a whole new world.

Fast forward 20 years. The day was October 24, 1995, Nini's first great grandchild, Tatum Rebekah Nugent, discovered America. November 14, 1996, Johnson Saunders Covert became her first great grandson. Only to be followed by Taylor Baines Nugent, Claudia Robinson Covert, Eloise Patrick Turpin McIntosh, Tucker William Thomas McIntosh, Luci Bella Rogers McIntosh, Sophia Baines Brod, Isabella Taylor Brod and finally Madeline Taylor Florio. This is when I think that Nini found that her most favorite role was that of great grandmother. There was no longer a children's table— they sat at the table usually right next to Nini so that she could see them. The banging of pots and pans for a marching band parade were encouraged—by Nini. Christmas time at the ranch was just like it was when the President was alive—presents everywhere and great grandchildren putting on a Christmas pageant. The trips and discoveries now took place at the LBJ Ranch or looking at wildflowers. Nini loved swimming with the children. Nini loved showing them every square inch of the ranch. Nini loved just watching them—all with their beguiling smiles! She exposed all of us to a better world filled with the most amazing people.

As many of you know, Nini was the best letter writer. Not only in her abundance of letters but also in her words. So today I will read you a letter that I have written to Nini telling her about all of the wonderful things her great grandchildren remember about her.

Dearest Nini,

Oh my how I wish you were still here to see your most precious great grandchildren. I know that all of them loved you the mostest. When I asked the great grands what they loved most about you or their favorite memory of you, this is what I got:

Tatum, 11—I loved going to the ranch on Sundays so I could help Poppi and spend time with Nini. I know how much Nini loved being at the ranch and I loved being there with her. I will never forget when she came to read to my kindergarten class.

Johnson, 10—I'll never forget the dinner I shared with Nini and Coach Royal after UT [University of Texas] won the National Championship. I will miss lying on Nini's bed as she stroked her fingers through my hair. She loved my hair! I loved how Nini would come to my games. She even got to come to my championship baseball game. I love baseball but not as much as I love my Nini.

Taylor, 9—I loved how Nini would come to our camp closings at Mystic! I loved how Nini would always treasure anything that I gave to her. She even liked my scribbles when I was little.

Claudia, almost 9—my most favorite memory of Nini is when I dressed up as her at school to do my biography and she came to watch. Everyone thought it was so neat that the person I did my report on showed up! I also loved having sleepovers with my Nini.

Eloise, 7—I loved being able to read "Little House on the Prairie" to Nini while she lay in bed. I also love telling the story of that when Nini could no longer speak, Tucker declared that he was going to find her lost voice.

Tucker, 6—I loved playing the guitar for Nini and watching her clap and smile the best that she could. Her favorite song of mine was "He's Got the Whole World in His Hands."

Luci Bella, 3—I loved it most when Nini would give me hugs and kisses.

Sophia Baines, 3—I told Nini that it was OK that she was old—just like my doggy Bruno.

On Wednesday night after Nini had passed, Sophia asked me where Nini was and I told her that she was in heaven—and she looked at me and said "you mean like the Bahamas!"

Isabella Taylor and Madeline Taylor's parents have helped in their favorite memory with Nini.

Isabella's took place last Monday night when she leaned over Nini to kiss her goodnight and she told Nini "night night Nini" and blew her a kiss.

Madeline's parents will be forever grateful that at Madeline's baptism at the LBJ Ranch Nini was able to sign the cross on Madeline's forehead.

Nini, these children were so lucky to have had the opportunity to share in your life. No one could have asked for a better role model. You have led by example and I know that these 10, soon to be 11, great grandchildren will follow in your footsteps.

Nini, I could never put into words or pick one special memory. I will miss seeing your smile and big bright eyes. I will miss the drivebys that I would do with the kids in our pajamas. I will miss seeing the look on your face when John would read to you about baseball and basketball. I will miss spending weekends and birthdays at the ranch. I will miss Lyndon trying to convince you once more to take a helicopter ride with him. I will miss the ear that you would lend and the guidance that you would give—especially reminding Brent and me to take care of each other. I will miss the confusion that everyone else has when we would talk about the three Claudias and the two Nicoles. I will miss seeing the excitement in your eyes whenever a grandchild or great grandchild would call you. But, most of all I will just miss you.

Nini, I feel so blessed to have been a part of your life. You have enriched me, encouraged me, believed in me, been there for me, but most of all you have loved me.

Night Night Nini—sleep tight!

I love you!

Lucinda Robb

My grandmother was wonderfully pragmatic, candid, and funny. She once told my mother that if she'd known how her life was going to turn out, she'd have done two things differently: She would have gotten a nose job, and she would have insisted people call her by her real name, CLAUDIA.

I can't say anything about the former. I thought she was beautiful, and I loved the way she looked, and the way she smelled, and how it felt to hold her, but I think her nickname stuck so strongly because it fit her so well. Despite some early confusion among the British about the possibility of a Lord Bird, the name worked because she reflected all the very best ideals about what it is to be a lady.

There's never been a piece about her that didn't describe her graciousness, and that isn't a word that is much thrown around these days outside of *Southern Living* magazine. But she was gracious.

I have two examples of her graciousness. I had two grandmothers, but only one of them is famous. From time to time they would both attend the various milestones of their grandchildren's lives, and my Grandmother JOHNSON, without being obvious or doing anything you could precisely pinpoint, would always make sure that any courtesy, any honor or sign of respect paid to her would be equally extended to my Grandmother Robb. It was the way she treated people.

The second example is I remember hearing that Barry Goldwater was coming to speak at the LBJ Library. I was younger then, and for some reason thought that Grandmother JOHNSON might not want to attend. She said, "Oh, no, that's not right. I'm so glad he is coming to speak, but I don't want to be there. It might make him feel uncomfortable if he sees me sitting in the front row. I want him to say what is on his mind, and if he sees me, he might not speak freely." So my grandmother did not attend his speech, but she graciously hosted a special dinner in his honor afterward at the LBJ Library.

My grandmother was the most quietly confident, least needy person I have ever known. She had so many people she loved and cared deeply about, but she didn't require anything from you. So many times we need other people to do something to make us happy. We need them to give us a job, to admit us into their school or club, to give us recognition, or approval, or favors. Sometimes we just need them to hurry up and do their God-given duty and give you grandchildren!

She didn't need anybody to do anything to make her happy. She rejoiced and shared in your accomplishments, large and small, but she didn't require anything from you. She was well grounded, and literally drew her comfort and strength from the natural world around her, only needed a little more rain, or a little less rain, in the hill country of Texas.

Paradoxically, because she didn't ask anything from you, it made you want to do good things for her, to make her happy. My grandfather was famous for his persuasive abilities, for the Johnson treatment. She was his equal in influence, I suspect, but we'll never entirely know, because her touch, while mightily effective, was so light. She believed in, and appealed to, the best of people, to allow them to rise to the occasion.

Perhaps the key to her success was that she really didn't care who got the credit. She was just going to applaud your good deeds. Growing up in Washington and in the political arena, a willingness to forfeit credit is a rare quality to say the least. It took a lot of work convincing her to change the name of the National Wildflower Research Center to the Lady Bird Johnson Wildflower Center, and in the end, they only succeeded by appealing to her pragmatism. They told her she'd raise a lot more money for the cause with that name.

Late last night my sisters and I went to go see the tower which the President of UT [University of Texas] had lit up in her honor. After the first spot we drove to didn't give us a very good view, we decided to go over to the LBJ Library. I was pretty cranky at this point. It's hot, I'm pregnant, you mean I have to get out and walk! Fortunately, my sisters inherited far more of my grandmother's good nature, and they managed to persuade me out of the car. And I'm glad they did. The tower was a glorious orange, but far more rewarding was the sight of hundreds of people streaming toward the entrance of the library to pay their last respects. It was past midnight, and they came in singly and in groups, some with children who should have been asleep. They had come to say goodbye to a lady they loved.

Catherine Lewis Robb

My grandmother was a beautiful person who spread that beauty to everything and everyone around her. I know that you all are familiar with her beautification efforts, to preserve the natural beauty of this wonderful world and to plant wildflowers on everything that wasn't moving fast enough to get away. Like many of you, I see the fruits of her efforts and dreams every day, when I run along the Town Lake Hike and Bike Trail in the mornings, when I bike in the hill country or just when I drive down the road. In fact, I frequently find myself whispering "Thank you, Nini" as I run, or bike, or drive.

But, just as often, I think of her other beautification efforts, and that was the beautification of the human spirit and of humanity. Just as she was planting wildflowers and trees and cleaning up the highways, she was planting kindness and generosity, and grace. To me, her other beautification effort was in planting the fruits of the spirit, love, joy, peace, patience, kindness, generosity, fidelity, gentleness, self control.

So often, when I would bring friends to the ranch or would just have visitors in her presence, I heard from them again and again how very gracious and welcoming and warm she was. She made every person she encountered feel as if they were so very, very wanted at that exact moment. It was as if there was nothing that could make her happier than seeing you right then. And, not only did she make you feel special, but she made you want to make others know how special they were, too. It was as if her grace and kindness just washed off onto you when you came near. She made you want to be more kind and generous and gracious.

This same sharing of her spirit of grace and love, and joy, and kindness was evident in those close to her. We saw it in the faces and words of friends and family, of those with whom she worked, of the ranch staff and her agents, and more recently, her care-givers, all of whom were there loving and supporting not only her, but all of us and each other in Nini's final tender moments on this earth. These fruits of the Spirit have been planted in all of us.

My Nini and I have had a standing Tuesday night dinner date for the past 8 years. Although in more recent years we spent most of our Tuesdays staying in and talking or reading, for many years we went out to restaurants. Often, people would come over for a quick second to say hello and express their appreciation for something our Nini had done or just for being the person she was and she would thank them for their kindness. Quite often, as we were leaving the restaurant, we would pass a table and hear voices call out "Thank you, LADY BIRD" or "We love you LADY BIRD." That was her spirit. She caused people to break out into spontaneous thank yous and I love yous. What a wonderful thing.

So, Nini, I will miss you every Tuesday. And more. And, I thank you for all of your beautification efforts of every kind.

I hope that all who love her will work to beautify the land and beautify the spirit and make both wildflowers and "I love yous" flourish all over this world she so loved.

Lynda Robb

Mother, you gave voice many times to the hope we would cele-brate as we remembered you. Right now, that is a tough assign-ment.

You know I'll always honor you, rejoice in being your daughter and tell the funny tales that made you laugh, but in my heart I didn't ever want you to go.

And yet we gather to send you off on what you always called your "final great adventure," but at 94 you put it off as long as you could. We had time together to relish sweet days, to welcome my first grandbaby, and to make oh, so many memories.

But we knew the day would come. I always told you that so many would want to celebrate with you that you would have to arrange for a spring farewell so the weather would cooperate.

"It can't be spring" you said. "Because I don't want to miss the wildflowers." Mother, this was our best spring for wildflowers ever.

I told everyone who would listen that I just couldn't speak at your funeral. Not only would your death devastate me, but I'd be losing my best friend. And you were my best friend. I could tell you my secrets, my fears, my dreams, prefaced with "I'm telling you this as my best friend not as my mother" and count on your counsel as a friend.

Mother, you always thought of everything as a big adventure— a mantra you instilled in us. It was very good advice when we had to do something we didn't find appealing.

Your spirit revealed itself at an early age. At 13, you drove by yourself from East Texas to Alabama. As a teenager, you were unafraid to hop into a rickety biplane.

Along with your love of adventure was your puritan work ethic, something you tried to give all of us. I am not sure you ever learned to do "nothing," to just play. Everything needed a purpose. In the White House days I would have to kidnap you and drag you away from your duties so we could have a fun lunch at the Jockey Club or visit a new exhibit at the National Gallery. You would do it only for my sake.

The Great Depression left a deep impact on you, Mother, resulting in another of your legendary qualities—your frugality. We teased you about it unmercifully. Daddy used to say he couldn't reach you because "you were out shopping trying to save 10 cents on a can of beans!" You wanted to get three bids for everything. You wanted to hold on until 2010 so we wouldn't have to pay the estate tax.

Later in life, when you thought it frivolous to spend money on yourself, you justified the expense by inviting friends and family to go with you on your trips. Daddy had long ago accused you of having one foot in the middle of the big road, and from the Galapagos Islands to the wilds of Africa your footsteps and zest for adventure never faltered.

One trip was especially unforgettable. You rented a French chateau and treated your guests to a once-in-a-lifetime visit. It was most memorable because it turned out there was only one bathroom for all 15 of us.

One of your biggest adventures started before I was born when Daddy propelled you headlong into politics.

At the start, it was an unglamorous role comprised mainly of making sure Daddy had enough clean, ironed shirts and calling everyone in the phone book starting with the A's, to ask for their vote for Daddy.

When Chuck became a candidate for public office, I asked you what you had done to help Daddy. "Most important," you said, "I followed behind him telling everyone thank you."

In the early years, you sat quietly during his campaign speeches, smiling, and sometimes giving Daddy the sign that he was going on too long. Soon, at Daddy's prodding, you, a reluctant, shy speaker, went out on your own, campaigning. It didn't take long for you to realize that politics was part of the poetry of democracy.

And as your platform for change grew you were able to lobby for the causes dear to your own heart. Your love of nature, born from barefoot steps deep in the East Texas woods, found a voice in your tireless work for nationwide beautification. Your political courage as Daddy's eyes and ears took you through the South on the Lady Bird Special.

Later, at 70, in the self-described happy hour of your life, came the living tribute to your idea of "paying rent for the space you took up" on this earth. Your lifetime of advocacy for clean roadside views, for the beauty of nature, for sweet wildflowers, or as you called them "weeds without press agents" manifested in the creation of the Lady Bird Johnson Wildflower Center.

You found deep joy in nature, in almost every aspect of life, and oh, how you loved Luci and me. You spoke of the summer of 1947 when Luci was born as being particularly happy. You painted the scene for us—sitting on the screened porch with the two of us looking out on a succession of colorful flowers and the victory garden. It gave you the feeling of time standing still and of being under a spell of idyllic contentment.

Following your stroke in 2002, it became our turn to care for you, as you had for us. Family nearby you in Texas showered you with love and attention. I envied our daughter, Catherine, because she had a date with you every night for over 8 years, with you, Nini. Our daughter, Lucinda, planned a Texas wedding at the Wildflower Center so you could be there. And our youngest, Jennifer, took last year off from her job as a public school math teacher to be close to you here in Austin.

Luci's proximity to you was also to become one of my richest blessings. Her children and grandchildren surrounded you with constant love. Luci's tender care of Momma when she could no longer care for herself was born of the purest essence of love. Luci has earned her own place in heaven.

As you moved through your eighties, Mother, you portrayed your life as relishing every day, feeling like a jug into which rich wine is poured until it is full to the top and overflowing.

One of your ministers described you as being a vessel of God's perfect love. Your love for Him, like that jug of wine, was full to the top and it spilled over to bless your family and friends and those all across the country.

Mother, the angels are here to receive you now. As you always told us, "know you are loved."

Luci Baines Johnson

Mother would want me to thank each of you for coming today and I want to let you in on a secret—you were all her favorites!

Once I asked my mother "how do you want to be remembered?"

She replied in her usual self-effacing way, "Well, I made a lot of little lists and scratched them off."

Little lists, were my mother's constant companions.

Campaign schedules, thank you lists and an ever-growing Christmas list. Her lists were for community causes, businesses, and family, but they were all lists to serve others.

Sometimes I'd say "Can't we take time off from duty for just a few days?"

She couldn't.

Duty was her oxygen. But she didn't seem to feel the burden of duty, only the calling.

In the final years Mother let me cross her lists off. Often I would make a speech or host an event for her. While I could be her representative I knew there was no substitute for LADY BIRD JOHNSON.

I will always be especially grateful to my husband Ian for quietly helping Mother with her lists in big ways and small—managing our business, serving her Wildflower Center, and reading to her on ranch weekends.

We never succeeded entirely at weaning Mamma from the lists but aging became our ally. She finally gave herself permission to just spend time delighting in family.

Mother always said "Life can be separated into categories, the 'if only's and aren't we grateful'."

One of the most profound "if only's" was the shortness of Daddy's life. She was barely 60 when Daddy died.

Mother, for the greatest inheritance one can ever know—parents who adored each other until death I'm forever grateful.

When Lyndon, Nicole, Rebekah, and Claudia were young I asked Mother if she would take them sometime on an adventure without their siblings.

She tailor made an individual trip for each of them from the beaches of Kitty Hawk to the redwoods of California to the museums and theater of New York City! These trips meant the world to my children and to me.

But perhaps Mother's greatest gift to all her grandchildren occurred when she inculcated them with the desire to be involved and caring citizens by giving them a Christmas check for the charity of their choice.

They returned her love by working for causes she held dear in the environment, education, health care, and social justice, and with regular loving calls and visits.

Mother, for widening our world through travel, for teaching us life's greatest joy is found in giving our family is forever grateful.

The grandchildren say those who describe their grandmother in only gracious terms never played cards with her.

Nini, for your merry and mischievous spirit we are forever grateful!

Until the day Mamma went to heaven her passion was the Wildflower Center. She loved the natural world feeling a keen responsibility to nurture it as it had nurtured her. Family always said if you want Nini to carry your picture in her wallet make sure you get it taken in the wildflowers!

Mother, for your commitment to what you believed in, our world is more beautiful and we're forever grateful.

Mother maintained a close relationship with her employees. James Davis worked for her nearly 50 years and Mamma said "when James Davis goes I'll go." Staff was family for Mamma, and she was family for them. My parents had no former staff, just former paid staff. Every foreign trip and Christmas Mother gave her Secret Service a party.

She respected them professionally and cared about them personally. For nearly half a century they were with her and they stand steadfast still by her side. Would Mother's staff and secret service past and present stand so I can thank them as Mother always did?

For your lessons in loyalty, Mother, we're all forever grateful.

The last years of Mamma's life Lynda called daily traveling half way across the country monthly for long and loving visits. She was Mamma's first born—her kindred spirit, her link to the Washington world Mother loved. They just don't make more devoted daughters than Lynda.

For being there for Mamma and for me, Lynda, I'm forever grateful.

Tragically, strokes stilled Mamma's eloquent voice, failing sight kept this most literate of women from reading and atrial fibrillation sapped her boundless energy.

But we were fortunate to have the most able and faithful doctors, nurses, and caregivers to help ease these traumas. Would you all please stand so we can thank you from the bottom of our hearts?

My last years with Mamma were magical. We spent a part of nearly every day together. No longer on a public stage we made private times we both hungered for. I had so much fun reading to her, retreating to the ranch, widening our worlds at the LBJ Library, wheeling her around Town Lake and the Wildflower Center where countless members of her fan club stopped to thank her, or simply giving her bedside nursing care.

I teased her saying "Mother 35 years later you're finally getting a return on your investment in sending me to nursing school." She'd laugh from her head to her toes.

Because of Mother my reading list was more worthy, my conversations were more substantive, I exercised more often. I was always learning.

A few weeks before Mother died, I was taking visiting relatives to the extraordinary Blanton Art Museum. Mother was on IV antibiotics, a feeding tube, and oxygen but she wasn't going to let that deter her from discovering another great art museum. What a picture we were literally rolling through the museum like a mobile hospital.

Every Sunday Mother's faithful priest's visit began with communion and ended with Mother's applause. Mamma had so much to be frustrated about but she never lost her temper or her thoughtfulness for others. My church preaches the concept of grace. Mother exemplified it.

One of Mother's favorite comforts was a 5-year-old great grandchild's recording singing and playing "He's Gotza Whole World in His Hands." Mother seemed to have the whole world in her hands too, teaching me by example not only how to live but how to die. For these lessons in faith, Mother I will be forever grateful.

CLAUDIA ALTA TAYLOR, LADY BIRD JOHNSON, First Lady, Mother, Aunt Bird, Nini or sometimes to children simply "Mother Nature"—a woman with many names and many roles.

Mamma, by any name, we all will be forever grateful for you.

It seems right for Mother's eloquent words to be my last. The night we returned permanently to Texas from the White House Mother wrote in her diary and I quote, "A little past 9, I went to bed, with a line of poetry reeling through my mind. I think it's from *India's Love Lyrics*, 'I seek to celebrate my glad release, The Tents of Silence and the Camp of Peace.' And yet it's not quite the right exit line for me because I have loved almost every day of these 5 years."

There is a hole in all our hearts as we finally release you, Mother, for we have loved every moment with you.

MEMORIAL TRIBUTES

TO

FIRST LADY

LADY BIRD JOHNSON

PROCEEDINGS IN THE SENATE

TRIBUTES BY SENATORS

WEDNESDAY, *July 11, 2007*

The Honorable Harry Reid of Nevada

Madam President, inside this desk is the name Johnson of Texas, majority leader. That, of course, is the signature of Lyndon Johnson, who was majority leader, Vice President of the United States, President of the United States. I have the honor of being able to work from this desk.

Lyndon Johnson is a legend from the great State of Texas, the Lone Star State. He was a Member of Congress, U.S. Senator, majority leader, Vice President, and the 36th President of the United States. But just as important, for those who know anything about Lyndon Johnson, were not these honors that were bestowed upon him by others but the fact that he married a wonderful woman, LADY BIRD JOHNSON.

What a name, LADY BIRD JOHNSON. Anytime you read about Lyndon Johnson, you have to understand the power of his wife.

Caro's book, "Master of the Senate," has a lot in it about LADY BIRD JOHNSON.

My wife understands, I am sure, a little bit about what she went through. In the book, it describes how he would bring people home with little notice for dinner, and it was always available. Mr. Rayburn, the Speaker, came to their home at least once a week for dinner, many times unannounced except by the President calling at the last minute.

Today, America has lost this great woman. The greatest asset Lyndon Johnson had was his wife. I join my colleagues and all Americans in tribute to this great American woman.

I did not have the good fortune to know LADY BIRD JOHNSON. She died today at age 94. But those who did know her said if you were to look up in the dictionary the term "lady," you would find LADY BIRD JOHNSON's picture. She truly stereotyped a lady.

I believe it is fair to say that you did not have to know LADY BIRD JOHNSON—I did not—to admire her for the causes she championed.

(3)

As I said briefly, I have my own special appreciation for Mrs. JOHNSON because I have some idea of what Landra, my wife, puts up with being married to the majority leader.

He was a domineering personality, her husband. She was, during all of the domination he had—with his poking Senators in the chest and the things he is now legendary for doing—she was always the same graceful woman no matter the situation she found herself in. She was the same person no matter what the situation. She served during challenging, extraordinary times. President Johnson went through some very difficult times. She was always at his side.

She did not ask for the role of First Lady, but she embraced that role with grace and dignity.

As First Lady, she was instrumental in the Highway Beautification Act, which came to be known as "Lady Bird's bill." She had many other initiatives that enhanced our natural world. She was a champion for children with programs such as Head Start. Later in life, her passion continued, most notably in her work opening the Lady Bird Johnson Wildflower Center outside Austin, TX, where she will lie before reaching her final resting place at the Johnson family ranch in Stonewall, TX.

I can think of no better tribute to LADY BIRD JOHNSON than to close with her own words. She said once:

> Some may wonder why I chose wildflowers when there is hunger and un-
> employment and the big bomb in the world.
> Well, I, for one, think we will survive, and I hope that along the way we
> can keep alive our experience with the flowering earth. For the bounty of
> nature is also one of the deep needs of man.

My thoughts and warm feelings are with her two daughters, Lynda, whom I know quite well, and Luci, whom I know of, and, of course, Lynda's husband, our former colleague, Chuck Robb— who served with such dignity in the Senate. I had the good fortune of being able to serve with this wonderful Senator, great Governor of the State of Virginia, an extraordinary, gallant marine—and Ian, Luci's husband, and LADY BIRD's many grandchildren and great-grandchildren, all of whom she loved as only a mother and grandmother could love.

The Honorable Lamar Alexander of Tennessee

Mr. President, I would like to say a word about LADY BIRD JOHNSON.

We have had many graceful First Ladies in the United States, but LADY BIRD JOHNSON can truly be said to have been the First Lady of America the Beautiful. Her husband used to joke that he would hear rustling in the hall at the White House. It would be, as he would say, LADY BIRD and Laurance Rockefeller meeting to work on conservation projects. Her legacy was the Highway Beautification Act of 1965. She understood that we have a great many important issues in our country but that one of our great characteristics is the beauty of our country. Italy has its art, Egypt has its pyramids, and we have the great American outdoors. LADY BIRD JOHNSON knew that for everybody—not just the wealthy with big homes and big lawns—the beauty of our country was something to preserve. She did that, and she changed our entire national attitude about its importance. She brought out the best in us in terms of appreciating the beauty of America.

I visited the Wildflower Center in Austin, TX, before. I have seen the bluebonnets there in the spring, and I have seen how she influenced the flowers to grow in the rights-of-way on Texas highways. They even adopted the motto in Texas, "Don't mess with Texas." I am sure that is a legacy of LADY BIRD JOHNSON as well. But not only did flowers begin to grow along the rights-of-way in Texas, they did in Tennessee and in a lot of other places—in States such as Colorado. LADY BIRD JOHNSON has made her mark in our country.

Our family had the privilege of knowing the Johnsons and especially Lynda and Luci—Lynda married Chuck Robb, a former Senator. We were good friends. We spent many times together at Governors' conferences, and our children know one another. We express to Lynda and Luci and that family our sympathies. We know they have great pride in their mother as well as their father. But we think of their mother tonight as we think of her as the First Lady of America the Beautiful and remember her contributions.

The Honorable Ken Salazar of Colorado

Madam President, let me say I join with the majority leader in sending our condolences to the Johnson family and in remembering the great life LADY BIRD JOHNSON lived and the contributions she made to our Nation. ...

THURSDAY, *July 12, 2007*

The PRESIDING OFFICER. Today's opening prayer will be offered by the guest Chaplain, Mr. Rajan Zed of the Indian Association of Northern Nevada.

PRAYER

The guest Chaplain offered the following prayer:

Let us pray.

We meditate on the transcendental Glory of the Deity Supreme, who is inside the heart of the Earth, inside the life of the sky, and inside the soul of the Heaven. May He stimulate and illuminate our minds.

Lead us from the unreal to the real, from darkness to light, and from death to immortality. May we be protected together. May we be nourished together. May we work together with great vigor. May our study be enlightening. May no obstacle arise between us.

May the Senators strive constantly to serve the welfare of the world, performing their duties with the welfare of others always in mind, because by devotion to selfless work one attains the supreme goal of life. May they work carefully and wisely, guided by compassion and without thought for themselves.

United your resolve, united your hearts, may your spirits be as one, that you may long dwell in unity and concord.

Peace, peace, peace be unto all.

Lord, we ask You to comfort the family of former First Lady, LADY BIRD JOHNSON.

Amen.

The Honorable Mitch McConnell of Kentucky

Mr. President, when LADY BIRD TAYLOR met the man she would marry in fall 1934, her first reaction was to pull back. "Lyndon came on very strong," she said. "My instinct was to withdraw."

And when an assassin's bullet thrust her into the national spotlight on another fall day in 1963, she withdrew again. America remembers this remarkable woman for the quiet dignity with which she let a Nation and a stricken wife mourn the loss of a President they loved. And our first reaction to her in those days of mourning was gratitude.

Now we mourn her passing, after a long tumultuous life that was marked above all by quiet service and a love of beauty.

She was nothing like her husband.

Lyndon Johnson was an overpowering figure who filled up every room he entered. His personality still reverberates through these walls. But he always knew what he needed to get ahead in life, and he saw in LADY BIRD the tact and gentility he saw lacking in himself.

He asked her to marry him on their first date.

And soon the aspiring politician would marry this shy and pretty rancher's daughter. Sam Rayburn said it was the best thing Lyndon Johnson ever did.

LADY BIRD brought a deep love of nature from east Texas to the White House, and she shared it with America. Residents and tourists in Washington have her to thank for the natural beauty that surrounds us here and that makes us proud to call this city our Nation's Capital.

Millions of travelers and commuters have her to thank for the flowers that line our roads. The blues, reds, and yellows that light up America's highways are a living, lasting legacy to the woman who guided the Highway Beautification Act into law.

A friend to every First Lady since Eleanor Roosevelt, LADY BIRD JOHNSON stepped out of the national spotlight as quietly as she stepped into it, again respecting the national mood at another painful moment in our history.

She outlived her famous husband by more than three decades, and we didn't hear or see much of her over the years. But she'd remind us from time to time that she was still here, quietly accepting an honor for her husband or launching some good environmental work. And we were always glad to see her. She became for us a kind of living assurance that beauty and grace outlive tragedy and loss.

We will miss her. We mourn with her daughters, Lynda and Luci, and their families. And we join them in honoring a very good American life that was spent in generous service to family and country.

The Honorable Kay Bailey Hutchison of Texas

Mr. President, I rise to celebrate the life of LADY BIRD JOHNSON. She was one of the most beloved First Ladies in our Nation's history.

LADY BIRD JOHNSON represented the best of Texas and the best of America. Since the days that I attended the University of Texas with her daughter Lynda, I have known and admired LADY BIRD JOHNSON. I knew her as a woman of dignity, kindness, and graciousness.

Through the years, I have also come to know Luci, one of the most thoughtful people I have ever met. And, of course, most of us in the Senate know Lynda and her husband Chuck Robb, a former Senator from Virginia.

CLAUDIA ALTA TAYLOR JOHNSON was a Texas original. She was born in Karnack, TX, on December 22, 1912. During her infancy, a nursemaid commented, "She's as pretty as a lady bird," and that nickname virtually replaced her given name of CLAUDIA ALTA for the rest of her life.

LADY BIRD graduated from Marshall High School in Marshall, TX, studied journalism and history at St. Mary's Episcopal School for Girls, and graduated from the University of Texas.

In 1934, she married Lyndon Baines Johnson, another young, smalltown Texan, who would go on to serve our State in the U.S. House and Senate and then our country as Vice President and later as President of the United States.

In her role as First Lady, LADY BIRD shared her love of the outdoors with the American people, becoming the strongest advocate for improving our public spaces. She was instrumental in promoting the Highway Beautification Act, which enhanced the Nation's highway system by limiting billboards and planting roadside areas. I will never pass wildflowers on a median of a highway without thinking of her. She was also a champion of the Head Start Program.

Even after her husband left office in 1969, she remained active in public life and especially in Texas. She served on the University of Texas board of regents. On December 22, 1982—her 70th birthday—she and Helen Hayes founded the National Wildflower Research Center, a nonprofit organization devoted to preserving and reintroducing native plants in planned landscapes at the University of Texas. In 1998, that center was officially renamed the Lady Bird Johnson Wildflower Center.

As the U.S. Senator from LADY BIRD's home State, I have consistently worked to strengthen and promote her outstanding legacy. Over the years, I have worked to preserve the LBJ office in the Jake Pickle Building in Austin and to add the Lady Bird Johnson Plaza to the LBJ Library.

In fall 2006, LADY BIRD joined me at a groundbreaking ceremony for the new plaza. She was radiant that day. The renovation is still in progress and has now been scheduled to finish by August 2008—just in time for what would have been Lyndon's 100th birthday. The plaza will be graced by wildflowers which will serve as a tribute to LADY BIRD's love of nature. Each wildflower will represent the lifework of a beautiful woman who will always have a special place in the hearts of the people who knew her.

I am proud, as a Texan, that this Texas lady represented the best of our Nation. My thoughts and prayers are with LADY BIRD's family—especially her daughters Lynda and Luci. We all mourn her passing, but we should also celebrate this remarkable woman's life.

The Honorable Dianne Feinstein of California

Mr. President, I rise today to pay tribute to LADY BIRD JOHNSON, one of our Nation's most beloved former First Ladies.

LADY BIRD JOHNSON was a conservationist, an enthusiastic political wife, a shrewd businesswoman, and the loving grandmother of a close-knit family.

But she will be best remembered for her efforts to make America a more beautiful country.

LADY BIRD JOHNSON was born CLAUDIA ALTA TAYLOR to her parents near Karnack, TX, in 1912. Legend has it that she received the quaint nickname when a nursemaid exclaimed that the young CLAUDIA was "as purty as a lady bird."

At a very early age, she expressed an interest in the environment, and in particular, wildflowers—which would become a life-long passion.

A graduate of the University of Texas, LADY BIRD received a bachelor of arts in history in 1933 and a bachelor of journalism in 1934.

It was in Austin where she met her future husband, Lyndon Baines Johnson. The connection between the two was electric— after a whirlwind romance and courtship, the two were married in November 1934.

LADY BIRD was a loyal and tireless supporter during her husband's political career—usually behind the scenes—from Congressman to Senator, from Senate majority leader to Vice President, and finally, on that fateful day in 1963, as the 36th President of the United States.

And it is her accomplishments as First Lady that distinguished LADY BIRD as visionary.

LADY BIRD brought a dash of Texas hospitality and genteel charm to the White House during those first dark days of the Johnson administration, as the Nation struggled to recover from the tragedy of the Kennedy assassination.

A life-long lover of the environment, LADY BIRD JOHNSON is best known for the Beautification Act of 1965, which is widely credited as the Lady Bird Act. The legislation encouraged efforts to make the Nation's interstate system more scenic and limited billboards that could be posted along roadways.

So as millions of American families go on summer vacations, they can thank LADY BIRD JOHNSON for the beautiful wildflowers that bloom along the highways.

It was the first of a major legislative effort undertaken by a First Lady—and helped to transform the very nature of the Office of the First Lady.

LADY BIRD began her beautification efforts with the "First Lady's Committee for a More Beautiful Capital" in 1965.

Although it is largely known that the First Lady worked to have flower beds and dogwood trees planted throughout the Capitol, LADY BIRD also worked to address more urban societal concerns here in the District of Columbia, such as crime, public transportation, mental health and recreation.

And to LADY BIRD, beautification meant much more—it embodied a deep commitment to the conservation of this country's natural resources.

In her own words, it meant: "clean water, clean air, clean roadsides, safe waste disposal and preservation of valued old landmarks, as well as great parks and wilderness areas."

As First Lady, she was often considered a "shadow Secretary of the Interior."

When the White House Conference on Natural Beauty was convened in May 1966, LADY BIRD kicked off the conference proceedings by asking this important question:

> Can a great democratic society generate the drive to plan, and having planned, execute projects of great natural beauty?

And thanks in part to her efforts, the Johnson administration helped to oversee some 150 legislative accomplishments for the environment, including: The Clean Air Act; The Wilderness Act of 1964; The Land and Water Conservation Fund; The Wild and Scenic Rivers Program; and numerous additions to the National Park system.

LADY BIRD JOHNSON helped to ensure protection of some of America's finest natural treasures, including the Grand Canyon, the Hudson River Valley, and perhaps closest to my heart, the majestic California Redwoods.

LADY BIRD JOHNSON was also closely involved in President Johnson's civil rights efforts and his Great Society campaign, particularly on the Head Start Program.

She helped to ensure that low-income youngsters are given the opportunities they need to compete fairly and equally when they enter elementary school.

So she truly left her stamp as a First Lady.

After leaving the White House in 1969, LADY BIRD turned her attention once again to wildflowers. She was instrumental in launching the National Wildflower Research Center in 1982, which was later renamed in her honor.

The center has been central to helping preserve many species of wildflowers and plants, which are increasingly sensitive to the challenges of climate change. In fact, today, some 30 percent of the world's wildflowers and other native flora are endangered.

LADY BIRD JOHNSON was one of America's finest citizens. And she was recognized as such. In 1977, the former First Lady was presented with America's highest civilian award, the Medal of Freedom, by President Gerald Ford. And in 1988, she received the Congressional Gold Medal from President Ronald Reagan.

As Laurance Rockefeller aptly stated when LADY BIRD was awarded the Conservation Award for Lifetime Achievement in 1977:

> She's a role model for leadership responsibility for women. That's a big part of her legacy, above and beyond the environment.

LADY BIRD JOHNSON will be very much missed. And I offer my personal and deepest sympathies to her family.

The Honorable Jim Webb of Virginia

Mr. President, today I join people from throughout America in paying tribute to former First Lady LADY BIRD JOHNSON, who passed away yesterday at the age of 94.

LADY BIRD JOHNSON served as America's First Lady during one of the most tumultuous periods in our Nation's history. During the 1960s, this Nation suffered through the assassinations of our most promising leaders.

We were also bitterly divided by the war in Vietnam. With respect to Vietnam, the Johnson family was personally affected by the war. Many of us recall the White House wedding of Chuck and Lynda Bird Robb in 1967, and how Chuck Robb later distinguished himself as a Marine Corps officer in Vietnam.

And many of our cities literally burned as America struggled to end segregation and to usher in a new era of civil rights. On this last issue, in particular, President Johnson and LADY BIRD JOHNSON deserve historical credit for their leadership and political courage.

It was against this backdrop of political and civil unrest that America was especially blessed by the grace, humility and quiet determination of LADY BIRD JOHNSON.

Mrs. JOHNSON reminded all of us that America is at her best when we are civil to each other and when we treat our adversaries with tolerance and respect.

Of course, her legacy extends far beyond her grace, charm and steadfast loyalty to President Johnson. To a greater extent perhaps than any other living American, LADY BIRD JOHNSON was the mother of the modern environmental movement.

With her tireless efforts to beautify the countryside, promote conservation and combat roadside litter, LADY BIRD JOHNSON demonstrated the power that each of us has to protect the environment and make our communities more attractive. Again, we need to embrace her legacy today.

In my home State of Virginia, we have always felt a special connection to LADY BIRD JOHNSON. She was the mother of Lynda Bird Robb, who was the Commonwealth's First Lady from 1982 to 1986, and the mother-in-law of Chuck Robb who was Governor at that time and later a distinguished Member of this body.

During her frequent trips to our State, Virginians always embraced LADY BIRD JOHNSON for her warmth, grace, and strength of character. These were the same values for which all Americans held her in such high esteem.

I want to extend to her family and many friends my deepest sympathies, as well as my appreciation for her extraordinary life. America is a much better Nation because of the life and service of LADY BIRD JOHNSON.

FRIDAY, *July 13, 2007*

SUBMITTED RESOLUTIONS

SENATE RESOLUTION 271—HONORING LADY BIRD JOHNSON

Mr. REID (for himself, Mr. McConnell, Mrs. Hutchison, Mr. Cornyn, Mr. Akaka, Mr. Alexander, Mr. Allard, Mr. Barrasso, Mr. Baucus, Mr. Bayh, Mr. Bennett, Mr. Biden, Mr. Bingaman, Mr. Bond, Mrs. Boxer, Mr. Brown, Mr. Brownback, Mr. Bunning, Mr. Burr, Mr. Byrd, Ms. Cantwell, Mr. Cardin, Mr. Carper, Mr. Casey, Mr. Chambliss, Mrs. Clinton, Mr. Coburn, Mr. Cochran, Mr. Coleman, Ms. Collins, Mr. Conrad, Mr. Corker, Mr. Craig, Mr. Crapo, Mr. DeMint, Mr. Dodd, Mrs. Dole, Mr. Domenici, Mr. Dorgan, Mr. Durbin, Mr. Ensign, Mr. Enzi, Mr. Feingold, Mrs. Feinstein, Mr. Graham, Mr. Grassley, Mr. Gregg, Mr. Hagel, Mr. Harkin, Mr. Hatch, Mr. Inhofe, Mr. Inouye, Mr. Isakson, Mr. Johnson, Mr. Kennedy, Mr. Kerry, Ms. Klobuchar, Mr. Kohl, Mr. Kyl, Ms. Landrieu, Mr. Lautenberg, Mr. Leahy, Mr. Levin, Mr. Lieberman, Mrs. Lincoln, Mr. Lott, Mr. Lugar, Mr. Martinez, Mr. McCain, Mrs. McCaskill, Mr. Menendez, Ms. Mikulski, Ms. Murkowski, Mrs. Murray, Mr. Nelson of Florida, Mr. Nelson of Nebraska, Mr. Obama, Mr. Pryor, Mr. Reed, Mr. Roberts, Mr. Rockefeller, Mr. Salazar, Mr. Sanders, Mr. Schumer, Mr. Sessions, Mr. Shelby, Mr. Smith, Ms. Snowe, Mr. Specter, Ms. Stabenow, Mr. Stevens, Mr.

Sununu, Mr. Tester, Mr. Thune, Mr. Vitter, Mr. Voinovich, Mr. Warner, Mr. Webb, Mr. Whitehouse, and Mr. Wyden) submitted the following resolution; which was considered and agreed to:

S. RES. 271

Whereas Americans throughout the nation are mourning the passing of CLAUDIA TAYLOR (LADY BIRD) JOHNSON, who served as First Lady with honor and grace during the Administration of her husband, President Lyndon Baines Johnson;

Whereas Mrs. JOHNSON was born near Karnack, Texas and received the nickname "LADY BIRD" as a young child;

Whereas LADY BIRD JOHNSON was known as an excellent student and graduated from the University of Texas;

Whereas LADY BIRD JOHNSON met Lyndon Johnson in 1934 and the 2 were married later that year;

Whereas LADY BIRD JOHNSON was a successful businesswoman who helped build a small radio station into a multimillion-dollar radio and television enterprise;

Whereas throughout her husband's political career in Congress and the White House, LADY BIRD JOHNSON played an important supportive role as a partner and confidante;

Whereas as wife of the Vice President, LADY BIRD JOHNSON visited 33 foreign countries as an ambassador of goodwill;

Whereas, as First Lady, LADY BIRD JOHNSON earned widespread respect and affection not only for the tone of dignity with which she represented her husband and the Nation, but for her active involvement in efforts to serve the public, such as her work to improve the environment and to address the problem of poverty in the United States;

Whereas millions of travelers and commuters have LADY BIRD JOHNSON to thank for the colorful flowers that line many of our roads, which represent a living, lasting legacy of the woman who guided the Highway Beautification Act of 1965 (23 U.S.C. 131, 135 note, 136, 319) into law;

Whereas after leaving the White House, LADY BIRD JOHNSON continued to serve the Nation in many ways, including helping to found the National Wildflower Research Center, supporting the Lyndon Baines Johnson Library, and serving on the Board of the National Geographic Society as a trustee emeritus; and

Whereas, in addition to her service to the Nation, LADY BIRD JOHNSON was a devoted and loving mother to her 2 daughters, Lynda Bird and Luci Baines, as well as her 7 grandchildren and 10 great-grandchildren: Now, therefore, be it

Resolved, That the Senate—

(1) notes with deep sorrow and solemn mourning the death of CLAUDIA TAYLOR (LADY BIRD) JOHNSON;

(2) extends its heartfelt sympathy to Mrs. JOHNSON's family;

(3) honors and, on behalf of the nation, expresses deep appreciation for LADY BIRD JOHNSON's important service to her country; and

(4) directs the Secretary of the Senate to transmit a copy of this resolution to the family of Mrs. JOHNSON.

The Honorable Amy Klobuchar of Minnesota

Mr. President, I ask unanimous consent that the Senate proceed to the immediate consideration of S. Res. 271, submitted earlier today.

The PRESIDING OFFICER. The clerk will report the resolution by title.

The legislative clerk read as follows:

A resolution (S. Res. 271) honoring LADY BIRD JOHNSON.

There being no objection, the Senate proceeded to consider the resolution.

Ms. KLOBUCHAR. Mr. President, I ask unanimous consent that the resolution be agreed to, the preamble be agreed to, the motions to reconsider be laid upon the table, and that any statements relating to the resolution be printed in the *Record*.

The PRESIDING OFFICER. Without objection, it is so ordered.

The resolution (S. Res. 271) was agreed to.

The preamble was agreed to.

MONDAY, *July 16, 2007*

The Honorable Richard Durbin of Illinois

Mr. President, we should all be so fortunate as to live a worthy life and at the moment of our passing have a person with the talent of Bill Moyers memorialize our time on Earth. On Saturday, Bill Moyers, the PBS journalist who served as special assistant to President Lyndon Johnson from 1963 to 1978, delivered a eulogy at LADY BIRD JOHNSON's funeral service. He read from a text which I will now have printed in the *Record*.

I ask unanimous consent that the eulogy be printed in the *Record*.

There being no objection, the material was ordered to be printed in the *Record*, as follows:

[The text of the eulogy is on page xlvii].

Mr. DURBIN. Mr. President, those of us who are fortunate enough to know Mr. Moyers understand what an extraordinary person he is. I hope those who read the remarks he made about LADY BIRD JOHNSON will come to appreciate so much more the contributions she made in her life. She was a gracious and caring person. Bill Moyers' eulogy reminds us she was also a person of exceptional courage.

I join America in extending condolences to LADY BIRD JOHNSON's family, to the family of our former colleague, Senator Charles and Lynda Robb, and to all those who mourn her passing, and I yield the floor.

The PRESIDING OFFICER. The Senator from Rhode Island.

The Honorable Jack Reed of Rhode Island

Mr. President, first let me associate myself with the comments of Senator Durbin about LADY BIRD JOHNSON. I had the privilege and pleasure for many years of knowing a dear friend of their family, my dear friend, Warrie Price and her family. She was there in Austin for the services.

Also, I had the privilege of serving with Senator Chuck Robb and knowing Lynda. I thank the Senator for recognizing those comments by Bill Moyers. When I spoke to my friend, Warrie Price, she said she had never heard anything as moving and as evocative and as fitting as the tribute by Bill Moyers.

I thank the Senator for including that in the *Record* for the American people to consider.

THURSDAY, *July 19, 2007*

The Honorable Joseph R. Biden, Jr., of Delaware

Madam President, so much has been said about the various parts of LADY BIRD JOHNSON's life, as one of our most beloved First Ladies, as a loving mother and grandmother, as the mother of the conservation movement, and as a skilled businesswoman. But there is another aspect all of us in this body appreciate, and that is her mark on this Chamber.

Before the Johnsons left Washington in January 1969, they came to the Capitol to say farewell. And the ever gracious LADY BIRD JOHNSON, who had watched her husband serve as a Senator and a majority leader, said:

> When we say goodbye to Washington, the address of 1600 Pennsylvania Avenue was a small span of time for us in comparison to the years that we spent closely affiliated with this building.

She knew how to use this building. She was the first First Lady to ever undertake a major legislative effort—the Highway Beautification Act of 1965. Four decades later, her efforts still bloom on our highways in every region of this country, and in this city.

She did what each of us, and all of us combined, come here to do—leave America better than we found it. Her achievement is all the more remarkable because it was a trying period in our Nation's history. A President had been assassinated, we were divided by Vietnam, there were riots in our cities over desegregation.

But she understood nature belongs to every single one of us, and we have an obligation to pay nature back. As President Johnson said, when he signed the law:

> There is a part of America which was here long before we arrived, and will be here, if we preserve it, long after we depart.

As Mrs. JOHNSON departs, we thank her for her preservation. We thank her for lining every corner of the country with flowers that we all enjoy.

And we thank her for teaching us that preservation and beauty go beyond the wildflowers, to the need to deal with pollution and urban decay and other problems that are too prevalent in our country and world today.

Jill and I are thinking of her daughters, Lynda and Luci, their families—and, in particular, Senator Robb, who served this body so well.

WEDNESDAY, *July 25, 2007*

The Honorable John D. Rockefeller IV of West Virginia

Mr. President, when LADY BIRD JOHNSON passed away on the afternoon of July 11, 2007, the United States mourned the loss of a dignified and compassionate First Lady. Even though she is gone, she has left us with the legacy of her beautification of America. Through her diligent efforts, Mrs. JOHNSON was not only an advocate for the natural beauty of America but also of the beauty and strength of its people. Sharon and I extend our deepest sympathy to her daughters Lynda and Luci, their families, her friends, and all of those whose lives have been touched by her life's work.

As President Lyndon B. Johnson entered the White House in one of our Nation's most harrowing moments, Mrs. JOHNSON stood by her husband with poise and courage that helped comfort a wounded nation. Her service to our country would go even further as she became a leading voice for preserving and defending America's natural resources. Here in the Nation's Capital, people can't help but be reminded of Mrs. JOHNSON's vigorous work to adorn Washington, DC, with flowers, giving us an aesthetic that all Americans could take pride in and enjoy.

I have always shared Mrs. JOHNSON's deeply held love for the beauty of the United States, from the mountains of West Virginia to the plains of Texas. It was because of her commitment to the environment and the splendor of our country that the Beautification

Act of 1965 was passed. She strove to line our highways with wildflowers and still found time to enjoy walking through the national parks that she fought to protect.

In addition to her work with the environment, I truly admire her efforts to address poverty in the United States. Under President Johnson, the VISTA Program was enacted, sending out volunteers to improve the conditions of impoverished communities. I can proudly say that as a VISTA volunteer in Emmons, WV, I saw firsthand the immense benefits of this program for participants and for the communities they serve.

I will never forget her devotion to her husband, her family, and her country. I will never forget her passion fighting for civil rights and against poverty. Nor will I ever forget her determination to leave a beautiful America for future generations.

LADY BIRD JOHNSON, again, held my sincerest respect and appreciation. To her family and the people of Texas, I offer my deepest sympathies. Mrs. JOHNSON was a valuable public servant, an inspiration and a friend. More than anything else, she was an irreplaceable First Lady.

PROCEEDINGS IN THE HOUSE OF REPRESENTATIVES

TRIBUTES BY REPRESENTATIVES

The Honorable Solomon P. Ortiz of Texas

Madam Speaker, I rise with a heavy heart to announce the passing of a great Texan, LADY BIRD JOHNSON. LADY BIRD JOHNSON was the essence of a lady so much that it was literally her name. She brought grace and light to the State of Texas and in Washington, DC. She was a partner to President Lyndon Johnson in the home, on the campaign trail and in the White House. She made things around her prettier, around the environment, and she brought light and beauty to Washington, DC, to politics, and to our Nation.

She was so proud of the Department of Education bearing the name of her husband, LBJ, to illustrate her dedication to education. Her legacy will live on in their beautiful family and in the flowers and beauty of the many parks that were inspired by her all over the Nation.

At this moment I would like to yield to my good friend, Lloyd Doggett.

The Honorable Lloyd Doggett of Texas

Madam Speaker, LADY BIRD JOHNSON cared for all that is beautiful and vulnerable in the world. I think every child in a Head Start Program, every wildflower gracing our highways is testament to her service.

In Austin we think of her years after the White House, the Lady Bird Johnson Wildflower Center, our Town Lake Trail, which families enjoy as a result of her concern.

Our thoughts and prayers are particularly with her daughters, Luci Baines Johnson and Lynda Bird Robb, their children, who are themselves a testament to her tradition and public service. And at an appropriate time we would like to ask that the House observe a moment of silence.

Mr. ORTIZ. Madam Speaker, I yield to my good friend, Mr. Barton.

The Honorable Joe Barton of Texas

I thank the dean of the delegation for yielding to me.

On behalf of the minority Republicans from Texas, simply let us say that we join in our best wishes to LADY BIRD's family. I knew LADY BIRD through the White House Fellows Program. For those of us that were privileged to know her as an individual, she was gracious and charming and an absolute delight to know.

We hope we will do a Special Order tomorrow, but we all join our colleagues wishing the Lyndon Johnson and LADY BIRD JOHNSON family our sincerest sympathies.

Mr. ORTIZ. Madam Speaker, let me yield for a few seconds to my good friend, Mr. Gene Green of Texas.

The Honorable Gene Green of Texas

Madam Speaker, I thank my colleague from Texas for yielding to me. And I want to thank this House, Madam Speaker, because earlier this year we passed a bill and it has been signed by the President naming the Department of Education Building for Lyndon Baines Johnson. A lot of our goal was to make sure that LADY BIRD was alive when that was done. When President Bush signed the bill, she actually heard; because of her illness she couldn't be in Washington, but she heard the bill signing and the great things said about the legacy of President Johnson and the Johnson family.

And all of us share the loss of the Johnson family and the loss of LADY BIRD. She literally defined the term "lady" for those of us who knew her.

The Honorable Solomon P. Ortiz of Texas

Madam Speaker, I ask for a moment of silence in LADY BIRD JOHNSON's honor.

The SPEAKER pro tempore. Will all the Members and visitors in the gallery please rise and observe a moment of silence.

MONDAY, *July 16, 2007*

The Honorable Al Green of Texas

Madam Speaker, I rise to commemorate the life and outstanding works of CLAUDIA TAYLOR "LADY BIRD" JOHNSON, the former First Lady of the United States.

LADY BIRD JOHNSON was born on December 22, 1912, to Thomas Jefferson Taylor and Minnie Lee Pattillo. As a child, LADY BIRD was a tremendous student who expressed great love for classical literature before going on to earn two degrees (bachelor of arts in history and in journalism) from the University of Texas in 1933 and 1934. She married Lyndon Baines Johnson on November 17, 1934.

When Lyndon Johnson became the 36th President of the United States, LADY BIRD showed groundbreaking leadership in developing new opportunities for our First Ladies. LADY BIRD conceptualized and secured congressional support for the Highway Beautification Act, which President Johnson signed into law on October 22, 1965. This important piece of legislation ordered the removal of certain junkyards and overly intrusive advertising along our Nation's highways. She also championed the creation and strengthening of the Head Start Program, which has helped ensure that all children have access to vital early-childhood education, regardless of their parents' income.

After her time as First Lady, LADY BIRD continued to show leadership in the causes dear to her, especially the preservation of our wildlife. In 1970, she published her diaries of her time as First Lady, "White House Diary," which detailed her pioneering accomplishments and inspired young women across the country. In 1982, LADY BIRD founded the National Wildflower Research Center, which works to expand the sustainable use and conservation of wildflowers and native plants. She also served as National Geographic Society trustee emeritus and Kennedy Center honorary chair.

As a result of her numerous good works, LADY BIRD JOHNSON earned the Presidential Medal of Freedom in 1977 and the Congressional Gold Medal in 1988. These honors were well deserved and serve as testament to the exemplary life of LADY BIRD JOHNSON.

Mrs. JOHNSON's passage is a tremendous loss for the Johnson family and for our country. It is with great sadness that I pass on my condolences to LADY BIRD JOHNSON's family and friends, but with great pride that I honor her incredible life and accomplishments.

The Honorable Ted Poe of Texas

Madam Speaker, my grandmother influenced my life in so many ways and she educated me in the ways of the world more than anyone in my life, but to her dismay I broke from her staunchest southern belief—the Democratic Party. I don't know that she ever forgave me for being a Republican and during the 1960s, in the heyday of LBJ, she was aghast that anyone could be anything else. Despite my political difference with President Lyndon Johnson, his contributions to Texas as President may only be surpassed by those of his First Lady. This week we said goodbye to one of the finest southern ladies politics and Texas has ever had the pleasure of knowing, LADY BIRD JOHNSON.

My grandmother always said, "there is nothing more powerful than a woman who has made up her mind!" There are no truer words; and none that describe our former First Lady better. CLAUDIA ALTA TAYLOR JOHNSON, known throughout the world simply as LADY BIRD, not only changed the landscape of Texas highways, but paved the way for the next generation of women. She was the best example of the powerful role women of her generation played—second to my grandmother of course.

While LADY BIRD will best be remembered for her love of the environment and the preservation of our natural resources, she was no wallflower in the business and political world either. She was her husband's staunchest supporter and was with him step for step throughout his entire career, but at the same time she also carved a path for herself in the business world by turning a debt-ridden Austin radio station into a multi-million dollar broadcast empire. Her resume reads like that of a modern-day Superwoman. Among her many achievements, she played a pivotal part in shaping legislation by lobbying and speaking before Congress in support of the Highway Beautification Bill, or better known as the "Lady Bird Bill." She oversaw every detail in the creation of the LBJ Presidential Library, which became the model for Presidential libraries today, and served faithfully, and often in awe of her colleagues, as a regent of her alma mater, the University of Texas.

Like my grandmother she came from a generation of women who were strong and influential. They possessed the grace of an angel, but wielded a heavy hand in running their affairs—and those of their husbands' for that matter. Few women of their generation worked outside the home, but few men succeeded without the backing of them. Whether they devoted their time to their work or to their home, their influence undoubtedly changed the country we live in today. Texas Congressman Sam Rayburn, longtime friend of President Johnson and House Speaker, once told him that marrying LADY BIRD was the wisest decision he had ever made. Few people know that LADY BIRD originally told LBJ "no," when he asked to marry her.

Every spring folks will head up Highway 290 to see wildflowers; and every bluebonnet we see throughout the Texas hill country and every tree we plant here at home along Will Clayton Parkway is a tribute to LADY BIRD and her determination to "Keep Texas Beautiful." Her legacy and influence will live on forever. I doubt that Texas, nor our country. will ever know a finer lady and patriot than we had in LADY BIRD JOHNSON. As the saying goes, behind every good man there stands a better woman. May God bless LADY BIRD JOHNSON as she has blessed us.

And that's just the way it is.

TUESDAY, *July 17, 2007*

PUBLIC BILLS AND RESOLUTIONS

Under clause 2 of rule XII, public bills and resolutions were introduced and severally referred, as follows: ...

By Ms. EDDIE BERNICE JOHNSON of Texas (for herself, Mr. Hall of Texas, Mr. Ortiz, Mr. Barton of Texas, Ms. Pelosi, Mr. Hoyer, Mr. Reyes, Mr. Carter, Mr. Edwards, Mr. Smith of Texas, Mr. Lampson, Mr. Poe, Mr. Gonzalez, Mr. Gohmert, Ms. Jackson-Lee of Texas, Mr. Sam Johnson of Texas, Mr. Hinojosa, Mr. Sessions, Mr. Doggett, Mr. McCaul of Texas, Mr. Rodriguez, Mr. Burgess, Mr. Gene Green of Texas, Mr. Cuellar, Ms. Granger, Mr. Thornberry, Mr. Al Green of Texas, Mr. George Miller of California, Ms. DeLauro, Mr. Dicks, Mrs. Capps, Ms. McCollum of Minnesota, Mr. Conaway, Mrs. Maloney of New York, Mr. McCotter, Mr. Schiff, Mr. Serrano, Mr. Kind, Ms. Kaptur, Ms. Linda T. Sanchez of California, Mr. Michaud, Mr. Cummings, Mr. Kildee, Ms. Bordallo, Mr. Udall of New Mexico, Mr. McNulty, Ms. Lee, Mr. Van Hollen, Mr. Jefferson, Mr. Holt, Mr. McHugh, Mrs. McCarthy of New York, Mr. Farr, and Mr. Altmire):

H. Res. 553. A resolution mourning the passing of former First Lady, LADY BIRD JOHNSON, and celebrating her life and contributions to the people of the United States; to the Committee on Oversight and Government Reform.

MONDAY, *July 23, 2007*

The Honorable Danny K. Davis of Illinois

Mr. Speaker, I move that the House suspend the rules and agree to the resolution (H. Res. 553) mourning the passing of former First Lady, LADY BIRD JOHNSON, and celebrating her life and contributions to the people of the United States.

The Clerk read the title of the resolution.

The text of the resolution is as follows:

H. RES. 553

Whereas LADY BIRD JOHNSON was born CLAUDIA ALTA TAYLOR in Karnack, Texas on December 22, 1912, the daughter of Minnie Pattillo Taylor and Thomas Jefferson Taylor;

Whereas LADY BIRD JOHNSON received her nickname "LADY BIRD" from a nurse who thought she was as "purty as a lady bird";

Whereas LADY BIRD JOHNSON was known for her academic accomplishments, graduating from high school at 15 years of age and graduating from the University of Texas in Austin in 1933 as one of the top 10 students in her class;

Whereas LADY BIRD JOHNSON married President Lyndon Baines Johnson on November 17, 1934;

Whereas LADY BIRD JOHNSON was a dedicated wife to President Johnson and a devoted mother to their two daughters, Lynda Bird Johnson and Luci Baines Johnson;

Whereas LADY BIRD JOHNSON served with honor and dedication as the wife of President Johnson throughout his service as a congressional secretary, United States Representative, United States Senator, Vice President of the United States, and President of the United States;

Whereas LADY BIRD JOHNSON was known for expanding the position of First Lady by taking a visible role in President Johnson's administration;

Whereas LADY BIRD JOHNSON served as President Johnson's personal adviser throughout his career, and was a champion of civil rights and programs for children and the poor, including the educational Head Start programs;

Whereas LADY BIRD JOHNSON was known for her passion for environmental causes and the preservation of native plants and wildflowers;

Whereas LADY BIRD JOHNSON paved the way for the environmental movement of the 1970s through her efforts to replace urban blight with flowers and trees;

Whereas LADY BIRD JOHNSON established the [C]apital [B]eautification [P]roject and played a major role in the passage of the 1965 Highway Beautification Act, which was the first major legislative campaign initiated by a First Lady;

Whereas LADY BIRD JOHNSON and President Johnson retired to their ranch located near Austin, Texas following the completion of President Johnson's term as President;

Whereas LADY BIRD JOHNSON continued her dedication to education through her service on the Board of Regents for the University of Texas and through her work planning the Lyndon B. Johnson Library and Museum at the University of Texas in Austin;

Whereas LADY BIRD JOHNSON was awarded the Medal of Freedom in 1977 and the Congressional Gold Medal in 1988;

Whereas LADY BIRD JOHNSON co-founded the Lady Bird Johnson Wildflower Center in 1982 in order to protect and preserve North America's native plants and natural landscapes;

Whereas LADY BIRD JOHNSON leaves behind an honorable legacy that represents her gentle nature and strong spirit th[r]ough her dedication to her family and her passion for the environment; and

Whereas LADY BIRD JOHNSON died on July 11, 2007, at 94 years of age at her home in Austin, Texas, and was survived by her 2 daughters, 7 grandchildren, and 10 greatgrandchildren: Now, therefore, be it

Resolved, That the House of Representatives mourns the passing of former First Lady, LADY BIRD JOHNSON, and celebrates her life and contributions to the people of the United States.

The SPEAKER pro tempore. Pursuant to the rule, the gentleman from Illinois (Mr. Davis) and the gentleman from Tennessee (Mr. Duncan) each will control 20 minutes.

The Chair recognizes the gentleman from Illinois.

The Honorable Danny K. Davis of Illinois

Mr. Speaker, I yield myself such time as I may consume.

As a member of the House Committee on Oversight and Government Reform, I'm pleased to join my colleague in the consideration of H. Res. 553, a bill that mourns the passing of former First Lady, LADY BIRD JOHNSON, and celebrates her life contributions and achievements.

H. Res. 553, which has 58 cosponsors, was introduced by Representative Eddie Bernice Johnson on July 17, 2007. H. Res. 553 was reported from the Oversight Committee on July 19, 2007, by a voice vote.

Mr. Speaker, I commend my colleague and Representative Eddie Bernice Johnson for seeking to honor the former First Lady, LADY BIRD JOHNSON, and celebrating her life contributions to the people of the United States.

I urge swift passage of this bill.

Mr. Speaker, I reserve the balance of my time.

The Honorable John J. Duncan, Jr., of Tennessee

Mr. Speaker, I yield myself such time as I may consume.

Mr. Speaker, it is certainly a pleasure to honor a remarkable First Lady and great conservationist, LADY BIRD JOHNSON. And it is with much sadness that the House continues to note her recent passing.

Born in 1912 in Karnack, TX, in an era when women were not expected to accomplish great things, Mrs. JOHNSON came to represent strength of character that was the hallmark of her life.

After graduating from the University of Texas in 1933, she married Lyndon Baines Johnson. Mrs. JOHNSON became the mother of two daughters, certainly her most important work, Lynda Bird and Luci Baines Johnson. She spent the next few decades raising her children and supporting her husband in his political career, which, of course, led him to the Presidency. She was a trusting sounding board for her husband through all his years in the House and Senate and in the White House.

Mrs. JOHNSON led a nationwide effort to call attention to the beauty and the goal of highlighting historical sites and highways by planting flowering plants and wildflowers. While First Lady, she visited numerous public sites and scenic areas, thus bringing local and national attention to her beautification and conservation initiatives.

As we all have seen each spring in Washington, Mrs. JOHNSON has left a lasting legacy for all American and foreign visitors to this great city, who can now see incredible numbers of flowers throughout the area. She not only helped beautify Washington, but was also responsible for the 1965 Highway Beautification Act, calling for control of outdoor advertising, as well as the clean-up of junkyards along the national highways.

It is partly because of her efforts that we now have the Surface Transportation and Uniform Relocation Assistance Act of 1987, requiring at least one-quarter of 1 percent of funds expended for landscaping projects in the highway system to be used to plant native flowers, plants and trees.

After leaving Washington, Mrs. JOHNSON enthusiastically continued her conservation efforts throughout her beloved home State of Texas right up until the date of her death on July 11, 2007.

I urge my colleagues to please join me in honoring this great woman of Texas and First Lady of the United States, LADY BIRD JOHNSON, for her untiring efforts in educating a Nation on the benefits of conservation and beautification throughout her lifetime.

Mr. Speaker, I reserve the balance of my time.

Mr. DAVIS of Illinois. Mr. Speaker, I am pleased to yield 2 minutes to the author and sponsor of this resolution, the gentlewoman from Texas, Representative Eddie Bernice Johnson.

The Honorable Eddie Bernice Johnson of Texas

Mr. Speaker, let me thank these two distinguished gentlemen on the floor, Mr. Davis of Illinois and Mr. Duncan of Tennessee, for helping us with this today.

I rise today to honor the life and accomplishments of LADY BIRD JOHNSON. I would like to thank my colleagues Mr. Hall, Mr. Barton and Mr. Ortiz for their sponsorship, and the entire Texas delegation for joining me in sponsoring and honoring Mrs. JOHNSON.

Mrs. JOHNSON was known as a woman of class and integrity. She was strong in spirit and always represented herself with dignity and grace.

For decades LADY BIRD JOHNSON served with honor and dedication as the wife of President Lyndon Baines Johnson, throughout his service as a staffer to Representative Kleberg, as he served in the U.S. House of Representatives, as a U.S. Senator, as Vice President, and as President of the United States. She served as President Johnson's personal adviser throughout his career and was known for expanding the position of the First Lady by taking a visible role in President Johnson's administration.

LADY BIRD JOHNSON dedicated much of her life to the preservation of our environment. Perhaps she could be considered the first environmentalist in this era. This passion led her to create the Capital Beautification Project to improve physical conditions in Washington, DC, both for residents and tourists. Her efforts inspired similar programs throughout the country. She also played a major role in the passage of the 1965 Highway Beautification Act. This was the first legislative campaign begun by a First Lady. The trees and flowers we see along our American highways today are a testament to her work and her dedication.

After leaving Washington, President and Mrs. JOHNSON moved back to Austin, TX, where Mrs. JOHNSON continued to work for environmental causes. And that is, perhaps, the most environmentally sensitive city in Texas right now. Today we can all admire her legacy through the Lady Bird Johnson Wildflower Center in Austin, TX.

Mrs. JOHNSON died on July 11, 2007, at the age of 94 at her home in Austin, and was survived by her 2 daughters, 7 grandchildren, and 10 great-grandchildren.

I would like to extend my deepest condolences to the Johnson family. I urge my colleagues to support this resolution to honor LADY BIRD JOHNSON's incredible life and legacy.

Mr. DAVIS of Illinois. Mr. Speaker, I know that Representative Gene Green had intended to be here. Unfortunately, he hasn't been able to make it yet.

It is my pleasure to yield 1 minute to Representative Chet Edwards from the 17th District of Texas.

The Honorable Chet Edwards of Texas

Mr. Speaker, LADY BIRD JOHNSON was a true Texas treasure. She graced the Lone Star State, our Nation, and the world with her beauty and grace.

While she is no longer with us, the masterpiece of her vision can be seen along the highways and byways of America. LADY BIRD's wildflowers symbolize her life, a quiet, enduring beauty that will enrich our lives for generations to come. With our highways as her canvas, she painted with a brush of God's hand a landscape that brings peace to us in our day-to-day lives.

The beauty of LADY BIRD JOHNSON's vision did not stop with the highways and parks of our Nation, for she also envisioned a world not blighted by the ugliness of poverty and discrimination. As a partner to the President who fought for a Great Society, she helped make ours a better society. For that we are all her beneficiaries. I thank God for the life and spirit of LADY BIRD JOHNSON.

Mr. DAVIS of Illinois. Mr. Speaker, it is my pleasure to yield 2 minutes to LADY BIRD JOHNSON's Representative, the gentleman from Texas, Representative Lloyd Doggett.

The Honorable Lloyd Doggett of Texas

With heavy hearts, the thousands of Texans who participated in memorials to LADY BIRD JOHNSON, especially those who filled the streets of Austin, Dripping Springs, and Johnson City, attest to our affection and respect for her compassion, warmth and leadership. And with unusually heavy rainfall this year, Texas is literally alive with her legacy, the beautiful wildflowers along our roadways, and filling the photo albums and scrapbooks with children smiling in a bed of bluebonnets or Indian paintbrush for one family after another.

She knew a better America was one that gives all of its citizens an opportunity to succeed. And with the reauthorization this year of Head Start, more young Americans can access quality early education, ensuring that no child starts behind.

When my predecessor, Representative Jake Pickle, spoke on this floor after the death of President Johnson, he said that Mrs. JOHNSON was her husband's wisest adviser, and that their daughters, Lynda Bird and Luci, had brought "so much credit to their family and to our country."

Of her many gifts, perhaps her most meaningful legacy is her spirit of giving that lives on in her children and grandchildren. In Austin, her daughter Luci and her grandchildren, Catherine Robb and Nicole Covert, among others, give their time, support and leadership to causes such as SafePlace, Seton, the University of Texas, and the Children's Medical Center Foundation.

Mrs. JOHNSON promoted native species. They have strong roots and improve and beautify our land. The same, and more, can be said of the human legacy that she leaves.

The Honorable John J. Duncan, Jr., of Tennessee

Mr. Speaker, let me just close by saying it has been a privilege for me to handle this resolution on our side.

I know that most of us heard and read and saw some of the beautiful and moving tributes that were made to Mrs. JOHNSON in her funeral ceremony just a few days ago, especially the tributes from her daughters. And so I think this is a very fitting and appropriate resolution. I commend my good friend, the gentlewoman from Texas, Ms. Johnson, for bringing this resolution to the floor, and also my friend Mr. Davis.

I urge passage of this resolution.

And Mr. Speaker, I yield back the balance of my time.

Mr. DAVIS of Illinois. Mr. Speaker, it is my pleasure to yield 2 minutes to the gentleman from Texas (Mr. Rodriguez).

The Honorable Ciro D. Rodriguez of Texas

Mr. Speaker, I want to personally thank both the gentleman from Tennessee and the gentleman from Illinois, Chairman Davis, for allowing me this opportunity. I also want to take this opportunity to thank the Honorable Congresswoman Eddie Bernice Johnson for bringing forth this resolution.

Mr. Speaker, I rise today in honor of CLAUDIA TAYLOR "LADY BIRD" JOHNSON. Mrs. LADY BIRD JOHNSON was a woman of incredible caliber, a woman whose contributions of admirable causes have bettered not only Texas, but the entire Nation as a whole.

She redefined what it meant to be a First Lady. Along with championing the environment, LADY BIRD JOHNSON was a confidante to her husband, Lyndon Baines Johnson, and was invaluable to his efforts, improving not only health care but education. She, like no one else, understood the importance of early intervention when it came to education. Her efforts in Head Start to this day are there to show that Head Start has been a program that reaches out to these poor youngsters. Head Start has also proven that those youngsters that participate in Head Start are less likely to drop out than those that don't. She understood that from the very beginning.

LADY BIRD JOHNSON knew and had that Texas charm and wit. Her passion for the environment has left a lasting mark on America. Thanks to her tenacious effort in initiating beautification projects, the Nation's highways are more pleasant to drive on and the Nation's Capital is a lovelier sight. The city of San Antonio, where LADY BIRD married President Johnson, has also benefited from the First Lady's efforts.

Her highway beautification projects had a lasting impact not only in San Antonio, but throughout Texas. The Texas Department of Transportation says LADY BIRD JOHNSON's Highway Beautification Act that became law in 1965 annually dispenses over 5.6 billion wildflower seeds of some 30 varieties, including our State flower, the bluebonnet. LADY BIRD devoted much of her later life to beautifying her home and the State of Texas with admirable work.

With eternal gratitude from all of us, I ask you to join me today in remembering the magnificent work LADY BIRD JOHNSON has done for all of us. I want to thank her for what she has done for all of us.

Let me just say that every spring as we go along the highways and as the flowers bloom, we will remember her for what she has done for all of us. She now rests near the Pedernales River in Texas. Her legacy will forever be with us.

Mr. DAVIS of Illinois. Mr. Speaker, it is my pleasure to yield 2 minutes to another son of Texas, the chairman of the Intelligence Committee, the Honorable Silvestre Reyes.

The Honorable Silvestre Reyes of Texas

Mr. Speaker, I thank the gentleman for yielding.

Mr. Speaker, I want to add my condolences to LADY BIRD's family and tell everyone that while she will be missed, her legacy lives on in Texas.

I think her contribution to Texas gives us a unique insight into who the former First Lady was; a person who used her gifts, her position, her talents and her status to expand the world for everyday people, to make the world better for the inner city residents of the District of Columbia, and for the public that was traveling along the interstates of our great country, and, of course, for Texas.

She had vision and gave people a reason to be proud of their surroundings, to take ownership of their neighborhoods and communities, and to make them better places to live. This is meaningful and important on so many different levels for all of us that are Texans. In doing this, she was ahead of her time. She helped bring the cause of conservation to the forefront and drew our Nation's attention to the importance of creating and nurturing beauty.

I am honored and privileged that I met Mrs. JOHNSON many years ago when I was a college student at the University of Texas at Austin. I am proud of the legacy that she created and that she leaves with all of us. May she rest in peace among the hills, the streams, and especially the flowers that she so loved in Texas.

Mr. DAVIS of Illinois. Mr. Speaker, I simply want to thank the gentleman from Tennessee (Mr. Duncan) for his participation in processing this legislation. I want to thank all of the Members from Texas who spoke.

Mr. Speaker, I urge passage of this resolution.

The Honorable Joe Barton of Texas

Mr. Speaker, today, we honor the memory and celebrate the life of former First Lady, CLAUDIA TAYLOR "LADY BIRD" JOHNSON, and the contributions she has given to the people of a country she so dearly loved. I had the privilege of knowing LADY BIRD through the White House Fellows Program and as anyone who knew her as an individual would agree, she was a person of grace, charm, and an absolute delight to know. As a native Texan, a wife, a mother, a businesswoman, and First Lady, she emitted beauty through her presence and through her actions leaving a legacy that will not soon be forgotten.

LADY BIRD met Lyndon Baines Johnson in 1934 and in 7 short months, had captured his heart as he asked for her hand in marriage. Mrs. JOHNSON stood by her husband and supported his endeavors with a perseverance and tenacity that one rarely finds. When LBJ volunteered for naval service during World War II, LADY BIRD stepped in and kept his congressional office running and except for voting, served the need of every constituent. She again came to the rescue in 1955 helping staff keep things under control when her husband suffered a severe heart attack while serving as Senate majority leader. The former President once remarked that voters "would happily have elected her over me."

In 1960 Mrs. JOHNSON traveled over 35,000 miles of campaign trail as she pushed LBJ toward a successful bid for the Vice Presidency. During this tenure, she visited 33 foreign countries as an ambassador of goodwill. LADY BIRD again stood by and supported her husband as he became the 36th President of the United States and helped console the hearts and minds of an entire country as they mourned the loss of President John F. Kennedy.

As First Lady, Mrs. JOHNSON was highly involved in the President's initiatives supporting education and working to alleviate poverty. Under her own ambition, she created a First Lady's Committee for a More Beautiful Capital which later expanded to include an entire Nation. LADY BIRD was also the inspiration behind the Beautification Act of 1965 which transformed the landscape of our national highways. Never tiring in her life's work, at the age of 70, Mrs. JOHNSON founded the National Wildflower Research Center which is dedicated to the preservation and re-establishment of native plants in natural and planned landscapes.

LADY BIRD JOHNSON should be remembered by all as a person with elegance, grace and a tireless work ethic. She dedicated her life in service to others and gave so much of herself in support of her husband, family, and country. Today, as we celebrate the life of LADY BIRD JOHNSON, we honor her contributions to the people of the United States and recognize that we have lost a great American that will be dearly missed.

The Honorable Nick Lampson of Texas

Mr. Speaker, when Texans think of their home State, and frankly non-Texans do as well, a few key symbols come to mind. There is the instantly recognizable outline of Texas, along with the Lone Star, the Alamo, cowboy hats, barbecue, and so many other great traditions and institutions. Among them is the Texas State flower, the bluebonnet. The bright blue bloom of that flower throughout the roads and lands of southeast Texas is instantly recognizable. The reason why, of course, is that LADY BIRD JOHNSON led the beautification movement to protect and grow our State flower, setting a fine example of State pride for all Texans. We Texans feel the loss of the former First Lady when we think of this symbol, but as future flowers bloom, so too will her memory live on for our great Nation.

The Honorable Rubén Hinojosa of Texas

Mr. Speaker, I rise today in support of H. Res. 553, to pay special tribute to LADY BIRD JOHNSON. I am proud to recognize the accomplishments of a fellow Texan and a true Renaissance woman.

For much of her life, LADY BIRD JOHNSON acted as the graceful wife of a congressional secretary, U.S. Representative, Senator, Vice President and President. She devoted herself to her husband's political campaigns and lived in the public eye throughout the turbulent 1960s and Vietnam war era.

But LADY BIRD JOHNSON was also a scholar, a writer, a politician, and an advocate for education issues. At the University of Texas in Austin she studied journalism and qualified as a public school teacher. Later in life, she wrote "A White House Diary" and served as a University of Texas regent.

LADY BIRD demonstrated her remarkable talents for public speaking while on the campaign trail through southern States, where, as a product of an east Texas town steeped in traditional southern values, she was an invaluable spokesperson for the 1960 Kennedy-Johnson Presidential ticket.

While her husband served as President, LADY BIRD JOHNSON acted as honorary chairwoman of the national Head Start Program. As my colleagues may note, I am a strong proponent of the Head Start Program, which can make immense differences in the lives of underprivileged pre-school children by preparing them to enter elementary school on a par with their peers. Thus, I celebrate LADY BIRD's contributions to this invaluable program.

During this time, LADY BIRD JOHNSON has also been credited with holding luncheons spotlighting women of assorted careers. As a strong supporter of women's rights and pay equality, I believe that her efforts to applaud young women's advancements into traditionally male-dominated careers have had a profound effect on women's equality in general.

LADY BIRD was also an adept businesswoman who purchased a small radio station in 1942 in Austin and built a multimillion-dollar radio corporation. In today's society, young women interested in business and the telecommunications industries may look to LADY BIRD JOHNSON as a trailblazer and a success story.

While LADY BIRD's conservation work in our Nation's Capital is widely known, LADY BIRD's efforts to beautify our great State of Texas should also be applauded. In 1969, she founded the Texas Highway Beautification Awards, and hosted 20 annual awards ceremonies, where she presented personal checks to the winners. And, on her 70th birthday, she founded the Lady Bird Johnson Wildflower Center, to which she donated acres of her own land.

LADY BIRD has indeed left her mark upon Texas, as the namesake of a golf course, a municipal park, a walking trail, and a street.

Mr. Speaker, I am proud to join my colleagues in support of H. Res. 553, celebrating the life of LADY BIRD JOHNSON. She was a remarkable First Lady, businesswoman, environmental advocate, and trailblazer of women's rights. She has left a grand legacy of strength of character and service upon Texas and upon the entire Nation.

The Honorable Sam Farr of California

Mr. Speaker, the death of LADY BIRD JOHNSON was a sad day for the country. It was also a sad day for my district, and for me personally.

Mrs. JOHNSON also played a key role in drawing my father, California State Senator Fred Farr, to Washington. She successfully lobbied for his appointment as the Federal Highway Administration's first Highway Beautification Coordinator, wisely drawing his energy and insights to Washington.

LADY BIRD was a fervent supporter of so many of the values my constituents and I hold dear. She was a lifelong supporter of the environment, an advocate for preserving the special places in communities around the country. LADY BIRD visited California's Central Coast in 1966, where she dedicated Highway 1—now known to all as the Big Sur Coast Highway—as the first scenic route in the State. She even helped plant a redwood tree near Monterey's historic Colton Hall.

Mrs. JOHNSON was a passionate environmentalist. She argued against the blight of roadside billboards, instead calling for more trees and her beloved wildflowers. And many of the beautification projects that make Washington a gorgeous capital city were the product of Mrs. JOHNSON and my father. She was responsible for raising hundreds of thousands of dollars for the city's streets.

Mrs. JOHNSON's beautification projects and scenic designation programs were so important to drawing attention to areas that deserve protection. I encourage all of our communities to continue her work. We need more people like Mrs. JOHNSON in the world, more people who appreciate the beauty that is around us and who strive to preserve it.

The Honorable Leonard L. Boswell of Iowa

Mr. Speaker, I rise today in support of H. Res. 553 recognizing the passing of LADY BIRD JOHNSON and her contributions to the United States.

LADY BIRD JOHNSON, the wife of the late President Lyndon B. Johnson, passed away last week at the age of 94. We will remember this former First Lady as a woman deeply committed to her husband and his Presidency, as well as a calm and elegant figure during a tumultuous time in American history.

LADY BIRD took an active role during her husband's time in the White House. Before environmentalism was a part of American political life, she lobbied Congress to clean up the landscape of the United States. Through her efforts, the National Highway Beautification Act and the Clean Air Act became law and the Nation's Capital received a much-needed makeover to its landscape. After she left the White House, she founded the National Wildflower Research Center in Austin, TX, which was later named in her honor. The center continues LADY BIRD's efforts to preserve this country's natural landscape and beauty.

LADY BIRD also influenced many other policies and initiatives during the Johnson administration, including the War on Poverty, Head Start, and the landmark 1964 Civil Rights Act. She was awarded the Presidential Medal of Freedom by Gerald Ford in 1977 for her efforts both in and out of the White House. Through her numerous accomplishments, we will continue to remember her as a wife, mother, and passionate and dedicated American. While it is with sadness that I mark the passing of this wonderful individual, I am proud to be able to commemorate her incredible contributions to our Nation.

The Honorable Sheila Jackson-Lee of Texas

Mr. Speaker, I rise today in strong support of H. Res. 553, which puts the House of Representatives on record in mourning the passing of LADY BIRD JOHNSON, the former First Lady of the United States. CLAUDIA ALTA "LADY BIRD" TAYLOR JOHNSON was the wife of U.S. President Lyndon B. Johnson. Throughout her life, she was an advocate for beautification of the Nation's cities and highways and conservation of natural resources. The former First Lady was a recipient of the Presidential Medal of Freedom and the Congressional Gold Medal.

LADY BIRD JOHNSON studied history and journalism at St. Mary's Episcopal School for Girls, a junior college in Dallas. She graduated with honors from the University of Texas with two degrees—a bachelor's degree in history in 1933 and a bachelor's degree in journalism in 1934—a time when women were hard pressed to have a career of their own, let alone a college education. Her goal was to become a reporter but her media career was deferred when a friend in Austin introduced her to Lyndon Baines Johnson, a young up-and-coming political hopeful.

On their first date, which was breakfast the next morning at the Driskill Hotel and a long drive in the country, Lyndon Johnson proposed. LADY BIRD did not want to rush into marriage, but Lyndon Johnson was persistent and did not want to wait. The couple married on November 17, 1934, at Saint Mark's Episcopal Church in San Antonio, TX.

Three years later, when Lyndon decided to run for Congress from Texas' 10th District in the hill country, LADY BIRD provided the money to launch his campaign. She took $10,000 of her inheritance from her mother's estate to help start his political career. They had two daughters, Lynda (born in 1944), whose husband Charles S. Robb went on to become Governor of Virginia and a U.S. Senator, and Luci (born in 1947), who married, first, Pat Nugent and, second, Ian Turpin.

As First Lady, LADY BIRD JOHNSON started a Capital Beautification Project (Society for a More Beautiful National Capital) to improve physical conditions in Washington, DC, both for residents and tourists. Her efforts inspired similar programs throughout the country. She was also instrumental in promoting the Highway Beautification Act, which sought to beautify the Nation's highway system by limiting billboards and by planting roadside areas. She was also an advocate of the Head Start Program.

JOHNSON's press secretary from 1963 to 1969 was Liz Carpenter, a fellow University of Texas alumna. Carpenter was the first professional newswoman to be press secretary to a First Lady, and she also served as LADY BIRD's staff director.

In 1970, "A White House Diary," LADY BIRD JOHNSON's intimate, behind-the-scenes account of Lyndon Johnson's Presidency from November 22, 1963 to January 20, 1969, was published. Beginning with the tragic assassination of John F. Kennedy, Mrs. JOHNSON recorded the momentous events of her times, including the Great Society's War on Poverty, the national civil rights and social protest movements, her own activism on behalf of the environment, and the Vietnam war. Indeed, LADY BIRD JOHNSON and her husband were champions of civil rights and were instrumental in the passage of the Civil Rights Act of 1964 and the Voting Rights Act of 1965. I know that her comforting words and her encouragement were part of the decision making of President Johnson as he made some critical decisions during some difficult times regarding the civil rights of individuals who had been discriminated against for most of the history of this country. Long out of print, the paperback edition of "A White House Diary" will be available again through the University of Texas Press in fall 2007.

She was acquainted with a long span of fellow First Ladies, from Eleanor Roosevelt to Laura Bush, and was protected by the U.S. Secret Service for 44 years, longer than anyone else in history.

LADY BIRD JOHNSON was awarded the Presidential Medal of Freedom by Gerald Ford on January 10, 1977. The citation for her medal read:

> One of America's great First Ladies, she claimed her own place in the hearts and history of the American people. In councils of power or in homes of the poor, she made government human with her unique compassion and

her grace, warmth and wisdom. Her leadership transformed the American landscape and preserved its natural beauty as a national treasure.

JOHNSON then received the Congressional Gold Medal on May 8, 1984. In addition to the Lady Bird Johnson Wildflower Center, her name has been lent to the Lady Bird Johnson Park on Columbia Island in Washington, DC, which was founded as a result of her efforts as First Lady to beautify the Capital.

After former President Johnson died in 1973, LADY BIRD JOHNSON remained in the public eye, honoring her husband and other Presidents. In the 1970s, she focused her attention on the Austin riverfront area through her involvement in the Town Lake Beautification Project. From 1971 to 1978, Mrs. JOHNSON served on the board of regents for the University of Texas system.

On December 22, 1982 (her 70th birthday), she and actress Helen Hayes founded the National Wildflower Research Center, a nonprofit organization devoted to preserving and reintroducing native plants in planned landscapes, located east of Austin, TX. The center opened a new facility southwest of Austin on La Crosse Avenue in 1994. It was officially renamed the Lady Bird Johnson Wildflower Center in 1998. On June 20, 2006, the University of Texas at Austin announced plans to incorporate the 279-acre Wildflower Center into the university.

For 20 years LADY BIRD JOHNSON spent her summers on the island of Martha's Vineyard renting the home of Charles Guggenheim for many of those years. She said she had greatly appreciated the island's natural beauty and flowers.

On October 13, 2006, LADY BIRD JOHNSON made a rare public appearance at the renovation announcement of the Lyndon Baines Johnson Library and Museum. Sitting in a wheelchair and showing signs of recent health problems, LADY BIRD seemed engaged and alert, and clapped along with those present at the ceremony.

Mr. Speaker, in the last year the State of Texas has lost several of its greatest sons and daughters: Governor Ann Richards; Senator and Treasury Secretary Lloyd Bentsen; columnist and progressive icon Molly Ivins; and now LADY BIRD JOHNSON.

The Lone Star State mourns the loss of our favorite daughter and it will be grieving for some time. But the memory of LADY BIRD JOHNSON will never be forgotten so long as the flowers bloom in the capital city of our Nation and along the highways and byways of several States, especially her beloved Texas.

I strongly support H. Res. 553 and urge my colleagues to do the same.

Mr. DAVIS of Illinois, Mr. Speaker, I yield back the balance of our time.

The SPEAKER pro tempore. The question is on the motion offered by the gentleman from Illinois (Mr. Davis) that the House suspend the rules and agree to the resolution, H. Res. 553.

The question was taken.

The SPEAKER pro tempore. In the opinion of the Chair, two-thirds being in the affirmative, the ayes have it.

So (two-thirds being in the affirmative) the rules were suspended and the resolution was agreed to.

The result of the vote was announced.

A motion to reconsider was laid on the table.

The Honorable Solomon P. Ortiz of Texas

Mr. Speaker, I rise to pay tribute to one of America's truly great First Ladies, LADY BIRD JOHNSON, who taught all of us to appreciate the everyday beauty in nature, and who made it her life's work to spread that beauty to all corners of our Nation.

LADY BIRD JOHNSON was very much the essence of a lady, so much so that it was literally her name. She brought grace and light to the State of Texas and to Washington, DC. She was a partner to President Lyndon Johnson in their home on the campaign trail, and in the White House.

She softened the sometimes harsh edges of President Johnson, who came to office in the midst of great turmoil in our Nation. It was the age of escalation in Vietnam, deep fears about the Soviet aggression around the world, great angst over civil rights in this Nation, and both peaceful and violent demonstrations around the Nation.

In the midst of that agonizing dynamic, LADY BIRD made things around her prettier, and she brought light and beauty to Washington, DC, to politics, and to our Nation.

Recently, she was so proud that the Department of Education Building in Washington, DC, now bears the name of her beloved LBJ to illustrate their mutual dedication to education.

She was our Nation's first environmentalist, understanding that the aesthetic look of our Nation meant much to our citizens—and the survival of the human race would depend on our care for this planet.

Today, global warming has moved the environmental cause to a higher priority for governments and activists, but the matriarch of the movement was no less than President Johnson's and the Nation's First Lady, LADY BIRD JOHNSON. She loved nature and understood the relationship of Mother Earth to the long-term health of humanity.

Mr. Speaker, LADY BIRD JOHNSON very much appreciated that you lead this House of Congress and occupy the seat that is third in line for the Presidency. She deeply understood the importance of this government reflecting all our people.

Her legacy will live on in their beautiful family, in the flowers and beauty of the many parks that were inspired by her all over the Nation, and in the environmental movement that inspires us all to be better stewards of Mother Earth.

The Honorable Charles B. Rangel of New York

Mr. Speaker, the Nation lost a beloved friend and one of its most dedicated environmentalists on Wednesday when LADY BIRD JOHNSON passed away at the age of 94.

Much has been written about how the classy woman from Austin was a calming influence on our 37th President, Lyndon B. Johnson. When President Kennedy was assassinated in 1963, LADY BIRD stepped in and provided comfort to the Kennedy family and a grieving Nation. When civil rights legislation looked to be stalled in the Congress in 1964, the devoted mother of two took to the road on her own whistle-stop tour across the country, defending the administration's policies and goals.

However, her most lasting legacy can be seen any time you see the flowers bloom in the Capital or the colorful landscapes as you travel the Nation's roads. In addition to leading clean-up efforts of parks and natural habitats in and around the DC area, her advocacy helped push through the $320 million Highway Beautification Act in 1965. The Federal legislation provided money and other incentives to reduce the number of billboards and other eyesores along Federal highways and expanded local programs to plant wildflowers and other native plants.

Active well into her 90s, LADY BIRD JOHNSON was a role model for future generations. She broke the mold of what a First Lady could do, both during and after the White House. Her achievements and efforts with the National Wildlife Research Center that she helped establish in 1982 expanded the Nation's interest in the environment, providing a foundation for today's current green movement.

Her activism and graceful presence will be missed. Yet, her smile and charm will always be remembered any time anyone looks at the beautiful landscapes and wildflowers that she championed all across this great land.

The Honorable Tom Udall of New Mexico

Mr. Speaker, I rise today to pay tribute to the memory of Mrs. CLAUDIA "LADY BIRD" JOHNSON. Her humble and steadfast devotion to public service combined with her passionate concern for environmental issues made her an icon within the environmental movement. Modest and kind, dedicated and courageous, her contribution to American politics will not soon be forgotten.

As an advocate of natural habitat and wildlife protection, I greatly admired LADY BIRD's commitment to preserving and beautifying America's lands. My father, Stewart Udall, was Secretary of the Interior under President Johnson, and he credits LADY BIRD's several trips to the American West and the Rocky Mountains with igniting her love of the environment. Her campaigns to beautify our cities and highways, clean our lakes and rivers, and preserve our natural resources catalyzed many of the environmental campaigns politicians now pursue. LADY BIRD transformed Washington DC while her husband was in office by planting thousands of tulips and daffodils in parks across the city and creating a national roadside planting program. For LADY BIRD, wildflower beautification was not simply cosmetic; by expanding and bolstering diverse habitats, her projects inspired reverence for nature and the inherent splendor of our earth. She reminded us that to enjoy life, we must sometimes stop to smell the roses.

At age 70, she founded the Lady Bird Johnson Wildflower Center. She said it was her way of paying back rent for the space she occupied in the world. This center now leads the Nation in wildflower research, education, and project development.

Environmental work, however, was only part of LADY BIRD's public service campaign. As the first First Lady to have a press secretary and a chief of staff, she cultivated her own agenda. A staunch supporter of civil rights, LADY BIRD's strength, intelligence, and good judgment served as a guide and comfort for President Johnson. She also pushed for Federal legislation restricting billboards on Federal highways and fought for the Head Start Program. The projects she undertook always reflected her compassion, graciousness, and determination to make a difference.

LADY BIRD's compassion not only infused her political career but also permeated her personal life. Mother of two beautiful daughters, Luci Baines and Lynda Bird, LADY BIRD cared for her family with same exquisite grace she exhibited as First Lady. Luci and Lynda have inherited their mother's dedication to public service. They have supported a variety of organizations, including Reading Is Fundamental, the American Heart Association, and the Center for Battered Women. LADY BIRD's family and those close to her admired and emulated her loving patience, tender poise, and unending strength.

An environmental pioneer, a behind-the-scenes supporter and advisor for her husband, a loving mother, and a gentle soul, LADY BIRD will be sincerely missed. LADY BIRD was a friend of my father's, and our family will always celebrate the life of the extraordinary woman who gave so much of herself. In her various efforts to spread beauty and tranquility across the country, LADY BIRD has left this world a better place for us all.

FRIDAY, *July 27, 2007*

The Honorable Charles B. Rangel of New York

Madam Speaker, I rise today to introduce an article entitled "A Legacy of Her Own," in the *Washington Post* on July 13, 2007. This op-ed tribute written by Joseph A. Califano, Jr., highlights the legacy of LADY BIRD JOHNSON. LADY BIRD JOHNSON was instrumental in influencing President Johnson to support the Head Start Program for low-income children in the country. She was also an influential advocate of beautification projects in the Nation's Capital and throughout our country.

LADY BIRD JOHNSON's legacy has helped more than 20 million needy children since 1966 and her efforts have increased our country's appreciation for public space. LADY BIRD JOHNSON was one of our Nation's finest First Ladies and she will truly be missed.

MONDAY, *September 17, 2007*

The Honorable Sheila Jackson-Lee of Texas

... Mr. Speaker, I would be remiss if I failed to note one of President Johnson's greatest achievements and that was winning the hand and heart of CLAUDIA ALTA TAYLOR, affectionately known by all simply as "LADY BIRD." As First Lady, LADY BIRD JOHNSON started a capital beautification project (Society for a More Beautiful National Capital) to improve physical conditions in Washington, DC, both for residents and tourists. Her efforts inspired similar programs throughout the country. She was also instrumental in promoting the Highway Beautification Act, which sought to beautify the Nation's highway system by limiting billboards and by planting roadside areas. She was also an advocate of the Head Start Program. Throughout his life, LADY BIRD was LBJ's most trusted advisor and confidante. And our Nation is better for it. ...

○